The 'Did you know?' Nature Series

Mammals

of

Botswana

and

surrounding areas

Veronica Roodt Publications
'Did you know?' Nature Series

Published by Veronica Roodt Publications

Veronica Roodt Publications
PO Box 367
Hartbeespoort
0216
South Africa

Distributed by Veronica Roodt Publications

Tel/fax: (+27) (12) 549-1355
Cell: +2) 72 316 9712
Email (business): veronicaroodt@lantic.net
Email (personal): vericon@mweb.co.za

Veronica Roodt (personal) (+27) (12) 253-2883
Cell (personal) (+27) 072 634 9415

Written by Veronica Roodt
Sketches by Veronica Roodt
Photographs by Veronica Roodt except for the following:

Photo credits
South African National Park Board, pg 71 Aardwolf; pg 78 Striped polecat; pg 79 (middle picture) Honey badger; pg 80 African civet; pg 85 White-tailed mongoose; pg 94 Lesser bushbaby; pg 96 Aardvark; pg 98 Cape hare; pg 99 Rock hyrax (photo on left); pg 104 Greater canerat: pg 108 Woodland doormouse, Water rat, Red veld rat, pg 109 Namaqua rock mouse, Four-striped mouse, Single-striped mouse; pg 110 Spiny mouse, Multimammate mouse; pg 111 Bushveld gerbil, Highveld gerbil; pg 112 Star-tailed gerbil, Hairy-footed gerbil, Grey pygmy climbing mouse, Chestnut climbing mouse; pg 113 Lesser red musk-shrew, Reddish-grey musk-shrew, Swamp musk-shrew; pg 114 Rock elephant-shrew, Bushveld elephant-shrew, Short-snouted elephant-shrew; pg 115 All photos; pg 116 Peter's eauletted fruit bat, Angola free-tailed bat; pg 117 Little free-tailed bat, Schreiber's long-fingered bat, Cape serotine bat; pg 118 Yellow house bat, Lesser yellow house bat, Butterfly bat; pg 119 Schlieffen's bat, Hildebrandt's horseshoe bat, Darling's horseshoe bat; pg 120 Sundevall's leaf-nosed bat, Common slit-faced bat.
Burger Cillié pg 81 Small-spotted genet, (photo on left); pg 86 Water mongoose.
Shellie Roodt pg 20 Lion; pg 21 Giraffe, lions; pg 110 Brant's whistling rat (both photos); Baby baboons on back of book.
Leon Roodt pg 76 Black-backed jackal calling; pg 56 Springbok mother and baby.

Ⓒ Veronica Roodt Publications

First published in 2011
Printed and bound by CTP Printers, Cape Town

ISBN   978-0-9869926-6-7

Note from the author

The aim of this book is to provide a handy, easy-to-use guidebook for tour guides, tourists and students. My goal was to keep the book as 'travel friendly' as possible, ideal for game walks and an easy size to carry in a suitcase. A small pocket-sized book limits the amount of information and the size of the photographs, so a compromise was reached by limiting the number of pages to one page per animal.

The first section of the book (pg 3 to pg 26), provides information on the anatomy and physiology of mammals, in other words, how they are structured and how their 'insides' work. The behaviour of an animal is closely linked to, and often determined by its anatomy and physiology. The skeleton and skull are described in detail with photographs and illustations and there is information on skull muscles, dentition, locomotion, senses, reproduction, digestion and thermoregulation.

In the identification section (pg 27 to pg 120), one page is allocated to each animal. There is at least one photograph per animal, but where possible, two (male and female). Photographs of the droppings and skull and a sketch of the spoor are provided for each animal. The droppings were photographed with a match-stick for scale and the spoor include measurements. The skulls were photographed at the Ditsong National Museum of Natural History, Pretoria.

Distribution maps for the Southern African subregion accompany each animal. This will make the book useful in other areas as well. The animal names occur in English, Setswana, German, Afrikaans, Spanish, French and Italian (with only a few exceptions).

The basic information on weight, gestation, habitat, food, social structure, etc., is summarized in a separate block for each animal. The dental formula is also included in the summary and the formula is explained on pg 13. The 'Did you know?' section contains additional interesting facts about the animal.

The book is colour-coded for quick reference and the colour codes are indicated in the contents for cross reference. The animals are divided into six major groups (each with their own colour) - the non-ruminants, the ruminants, the carnivores, the non-carnivorous small mammals, the rodents and shrews and lastly, the bats. At the beginning of each section there is information about the group and a visual diagram of the orders, suborders, families and sub-families within the group.

This book is part of a series. The other books include 'Did you know?' guides on trees, birds, flowers, grasses, reptiles and insects of Botswana, and a seperate series for the Kruger National Park, South Africa. This book is the first in the series and the others will be released over a period of three years.

I had many unforgettable hours observing and photographing the animals, the skulls, the droppings and gathering the information for this book. I hope readers will join me on this thrilling journey of discovering the secrets and the wonder of nature.

Veronica Roodt

Acknowledgments

As this book is part of a series, I have been working on all of them simultaneously for many years. In fact, I was working on them even before the idea of a series took shape in my mind. During this time, so many people have helped me along the way. I want to thank every single person that has crossed my path and assisted me in various ways. I would like to single out the following institutions, companies and individuals: First of all I want to thank the **Botswana Government** for giving me the opportunity to work in Botswana, in particular the **Department of Wildlife and National Parks**. I specifically want to thank **Dr. Taolo** for his assistance. I want to thank the **Botswana citizens** for making me feel welcome in your wonderful country, especially the game scouts and the tour guides with whom I deal with most often. You inspire me daily to produce material that will interest more people to visit Botswana and which will ultimately benefit not only the country, but also its people; I want to thank **Jurgens Caravans** for providing me with an Explorer off-road caravan. The Explorer has revolutionised 'roughing it' in the bush and they have made it possible to travel with a mobile office. My sincerest gratitude to **Nico Pretorius** and **Elaine du Plessis** for their immediate willingness to help; **Outdoor Photo**, Pretoria, for providing me with camera equipment. In particular I want to thank **Hedrus van der Merwe** and **Wim van Heerden** for their kind assistance; Johan Kruger at **Honeydew Toyota** for his assistance in acquiring the perfect vehicle for the bush; **DFR Engineers Botswana** for providing me with the electrical equipment to enable me to have an 'office' in the bush; **Deon Roodt**, my brother, for his personal interest in my project and for his help over the years; **The Ditsong National Museum of Natural History** in Pretoria for giving me permission to photograph the skulls. In particular I would like to thank **Dr. Theresa Kearny** and **Dr. Shaw Badenhorst**; **Leon Roodt**, my nephew, for the use of his photographs, for sharing my love of nature and for his inspiration; **Burger Cillié** for the use of his photos and for his help obtaining the droppings; **Elaine Dugmore (Kalahari Kanvas) and Andrew du Plooy (Canvas & Tent)** for donating a Meru tent for my project; **Tim and June Liversedge** for their kindness, their assistance with my project, the use of their photographs and for giving me a home away from home in Maun; My sister, **Shellie Roodt** for the use of her photographs and for her assistance with business matters; **Edurne Martinez** for providing me with the Spanish names of the animals; **Juan Swanepoel** for his contribution with the lay-out of the book; My niece, **Janie Roodt**, for all her hard work in the bush and for helping me with the field work; **Lenyatso July**, my assistant and driver since 1994 for his help over the years; Most importantly, I want to thank my mother, **Ralie Roodt**, for her love, assistance and inspiration.

C O N T E N T S

NON-RUMINANTS (Setstswana names)

RUMINANTS

CARNIVORES

THE MAMMAL SKELETON

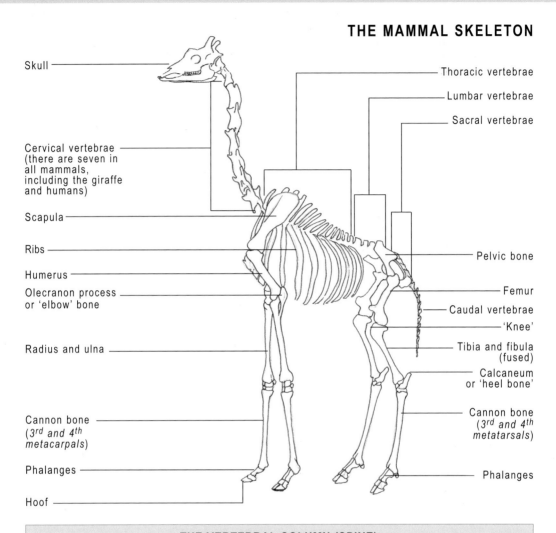

Skull

Cervical vertebrae
(there are seven in
all mammals,
including the giraffe
and humans)

Scapula

Ribs

Humerus

Olecranon process
or 'elbow' bone

Radius and ulna

Cannon bone
(3rd and 4th
metacarpals)

Phalanges

Hoof

Thoracic vertebrae

Lumbar vertebrae

Sacral vertebrae

Pelvic bone

Femur

Caudal vertebrae

'Knee'

Tibia and fibula
(fused)

Calcaneum
or 'heel bone'

Cannon bone
(3rd and 4th
metatarsals)

Phalanges

THE VERTEBRAL COLUMN (SPINE)

The vertebral column in mammals is divided into the cervical (neck), thoracic (chest), lumbar (back), sacral (pelvic) and the caudal (tail) vertebrae. The total number vary in different animals, the python holding the record with 435 vertebrae. A human has 33 at birth but four fuse to form the coccyx and the five above it fuse to form the sacrum. Humans have seven **cervical** (neck) vertebrae, as have all mammals (including the giraffe), 12 **thoracic** and 5 **lumbar** vertebrae - altogether 24. The tail vertebrae in animals are called the **caudal** vertebrae. The first two vertebrae, the atlas and the axis, support the skull and allow for pivotal movements - the atlas (first) permits dorsal-ventral (up-and-down) movement and the axis (second) permits lateral (sideways) movements. The ribs support the chest and the number varies from species to species.

Humans have 12 pairs, occasionally 13 and elephants have ±19 pairs. The first thoracic vertebrae of animals have long spines in most species for the attachment of the neck muscles and ligaments. Animals with really heavy heads, like the rhino, have exceptionally long spines.

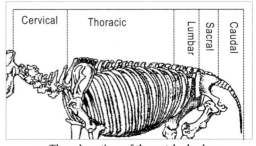

The sub-sections of the vertebral column.

THE PECTORAL LIMB (FRONT LEGS AND SCAPULA)

The scapula provides a firm brace for the pectoral limb (front limb) in the form of the shoulder socket or glenoid fossa. The humerus forms a ball-and-socket joint with the glenoid fossa of the scapula. This kind of joint allows mobility in several planes. The clavicle (collar-bone) is lost or reduced in most ungulates and other mammals that run on hard ground, so that the shock of the body striking the ground is absorbed mainly by muscles instead of bones. The humerus articulates with the radius and ulna in the elbow joint. This is a hinge joint allowing movement in one plane only (forward and backward). In all the *Ruminantea* (giraffe, buffalo and antelope), the third and fourth metacarpals are elongated and fused to form the cannon bone (see section on 'Reducing bones' on pg 5). The 'elbow' joint is the backward-pointing bone where the front leg meets the body. That bone is called the olecranon process of the ulna, which serves as muscle attachment for the 'forearm' muscles.

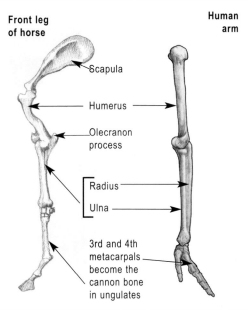

Front leg of horse

Human arm

Scapula

Humerus

Olecranon process

Radius

Ulna

3rd and 4th metacarpals become the cannon bone in ungulates

THE PELVIC LIMB (BACK LEGS AND PELVIS)

The pelvic girdle consists of the ilium at the top, which articulates with the sacral vertebrae, the ischium that forms the bony part of the rump and the pelvic bones. At the point where the three pelvic joints meet, there is a large socket - the acetabulum - which receives the head of the femur. The femur is followed by the tibia and the fibula, the latter of which is often reduced in cursors. The bone corresponding with our knee in animals is thus where the hind limb reaches the body. The patella or knee cap is retained in animals and protrudes slightly. The tarsal and metatarsal bones correspond with the carpals and metacarpals discussed for the forelimb above and are the same in the hind leg for the different animal groups. The part of the hind leg of an ungulate that corresponds with our heel is the section that sticks out at an angle - calcaneum or heel bone. The calcaneum is the largest of the ankle bones. It extends backwards from the joint with the tibia and serves for attachment of the Achilles tendon.

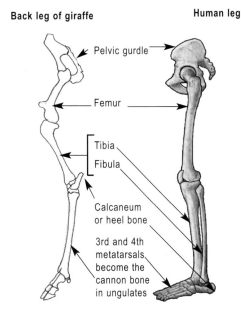

Back leg of giraffe

Human leg

Pelvic gurdle

Femur

Tibia

Fibula

Calcaneum or heel bone

3rd and 4th metatarsals become the cannon bone in ungulates

A BONE WE DO NOT SEE

A bone that is called the *os penis* or baculum is present in the penis of all carnivores (with the exception of the hyaena), rodents, insectivores, bats and some primates. A smaller but similar bone may be present in the clitoris of female animals in these groups (Hildebrand, 1988).

Baculum or os penis

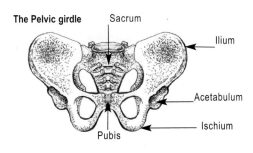

The Pelvic girdle

Sacrum

Ilium

Acetabulum

Ischium

Pubis

CURSORS AND SALTATORS

Agility, manoeuvreability and speed are essential for the large mammals as they need to travel long distances to find water and food. They also need to escape predation and in the case of predators, they need to hunt effectively.

Cursors - the hunter and the hunted need to run fast.

These animals, for which agility and speed are essential, can be divided into **cursors** and **saltators**. *Saltators* are animals that can hop and jump and are often bipedal, such as humans, primates, kangaroos and springhares. **Cursors** are able to travel far and fast on the ground and

Saltator - springhare.

include the predators and the medium to large herbivores.

Others: The mega-herbivores, such as the elephant, rhinoceros and hippopotamus, do not need to be fast and agile because of their virtual immunity to predators. Other animals that do not need speed for survival are the molerats and moles, which remain underground, the primates, which are arboreal and the pangolin, which rolls up into an impenetrable ball when threatened.

REDUCING BONES AND MUSCLES

Ungulates *Loss of muscle:* To obtain maximum locomotion, ungulates have evolved in such a manner as to make their legs lighter by reducing some of the bone and the muscle load. This can be compared to a car which can move fast in high gear but will have difficulty at an ascending angle. By putting it in low gear, torque (muscle) is added but speed is handicapped. Herbivores have forfeited some of their torque muscles and bones to improve their speed. They have thus lost muscles and bones related to twisting, rotating, digit manipulation and power. *Rotation:* By having the fleshy parts of the leg close to the body, speed can also be improved. The joints have been modified to act as hinges, allowing motion only in the line of travel. Compare the wrist of a human, which can rotate, with that of an ungulate, which can move only backwards and forward. Remember the 'wrist of an ungulate is what resembles the knee in the front leg of an animal (see illustration). *Loss of bones:* Some cursors have lost some of their digits and have fused some of the other bones. In the case of ungulates the third and fourth metacarpals (in the front legs) and metatarsals (in the back legs) have fused to form the cannon bone and the first, second and fifth digits have been lost through evolution. In the case of the zebra, the first, second, fourth and

fifth digits have been lost and the third forms the cannon bone, which is distally covered in a hoof.

Carnivores Carnivores do not have a cannon bone but they have retained all the metatarsals in most cases. The 'thumb' and the 'big toe' are shortened in many cases to form the 'dew claw'. They have also retained the ulna in the forearm and the fibula in the hind leg in order to retain the ability to twist and turn, actions necessary for effective hunting. Because of the power required when hunting they cannot afford to lose power in favour of speed and therefore reached an 'evolutionary compromise' by lenghthening the metacarpals and metatarsals and walking on the 'ball' of the foot.

Mega-herbivores They do not need speed and have thus retained all their bones and muscles.

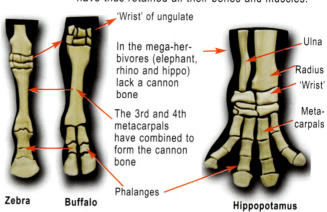

'Wrist' of ungulate

In the mega-herbivores (elephant, rhino and hippo) lack a cannon bone

The 3rd and 4th metacarpals have combined to form the cannon bone

Phalanges

Ulna

Radius

'Wrist'

Meta-carpals

Zebra   Buffalo   Hippopotamus

Front leg structure of the zebra, buffalo and hippopotamus.

ELONGATION OF END SEGMENTS OF LIMBS

Elongation of end segments of the legs A full cycle of motion of a moving animal is called a stride. The length of stride depends much on the proportion of the legs - the longer the leg, the longer the stride. A large body size does not mean improved speed, since this usually impedes it. To improve speed it is necessary for the legs to be relatively long in relation to the body and it is important that the distal (end) segments of the legs are equal to or longer than the middle limb segment. In the case of antelopes, it is the metacarpals and metatarsals that have lengthened most. Metacarpals correspond with the bones seen on the back of the human hand and the metatarsals are the bones seen on the top of the foot. As we have seen on previous pages, these have fused to form the canon bone. The hand or foot skeletons of ungulates are thus equal to or longer than the middle limb segment (radius and ulna in the front legs and tibia and fibula in the back legs).

WALKING ON TIP-TOE (PLANTIGRADE, DIGITIGRADE, UNGULIGRADE)

The length of the leg can be further increased by walking on 'tip-toes'. The human posture with the heel on the ground is called a **plantigrade** posture. Bears and primates that can walk well bipedally, are also plantigrade. Carnivores walk on the area that corresponds with the ball of the human foot. This is called a **digitigrade** posture. The ungulates and the equids have further increased their leg length by standing on tip-toe. This posture is called **unguligrade,** and is where the name 'ungulate' derives. Interestingly enough, the elephant also walks on tip-toe and qualifies as digitigrade. To support its enormous weight, there is a fibrous cushion of cartilage and fat tissue underneath the foot to act as shock absorber.

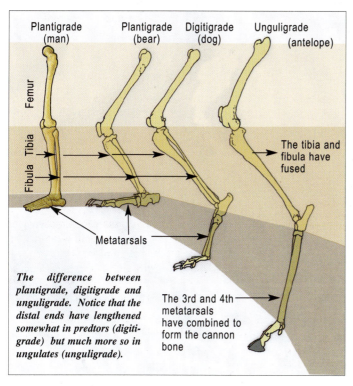

The difference between plantigrade, digitigrade and unguligrade. Notice that the distal ends have lengthened somewhat in predtors (digitigrade) but much more so in ungulates (unguligrade).

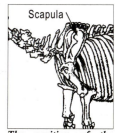

Foot of elephant.

POSITION OF SCAPULA

The position of the shoulder is another adaptation of animals that need speed for survival. In the case of man, the shoulder joint is virtually immobilised by the clavicle (collar-bone). The clavicle connects the sternum (breastbone) with the scapula (shoulder blade). Cursors have a free-moving scapula, having re-orientated it so that it does not lie flat against the back of a broad chest, as it does in humans, but rather flat against the side of a narrow chest, as it does in carnivores and herbivores. Herbivores have abandoned the clavicle completely and carnivores have reduced it to a vestige. Having the scapula on the side of the chest has the advantage of being free to rotate in the same plane in which the legs are moving, in effect, lengthening the leg and ultimately the stride. The scapula can rotate between 20° and 25° in some animals, such as the cheetah.

The position of the scapula of cursors add to the length of the leg.

The spine of a cheetah is very flexible, adding to the length of the stride (from Reader's Digest, 1974).

Equids and rhinos have a very rigid, strong spine, which supports the frame (from Reader's Digest, 1974).

Cursors also have the ability to extend and flex the spine. The galloping animal extends its back vertebrae while the hind feet are firmly on the ground to prevent the body from moving backwards again. The increase in body length adds to the length of the stride. Similarly, the forelimbs prevent deceleration as the back is flexed, also adding to stride length. This ability is well developed in predators but in the larger herbivores a rigid spine is important to support the frame, especially for the rhinoceros, zebra and horse. In the case of the rhino, the flexibility and strength of the spine is improved in that each vertebra has a slot at the back into which the next vertebra fits lengthwise. In the cheetah, the ability to flex the spine is so highly developed that theoretically, it was calculated that a cheetah can run almost 10km/h without any legs at all in 'looper-worm' fashion (Hildebrand, 1988). The speed of a cheetah is further enhanced by the non-retractable claws. They have the same purpose as the spikes on running shoes, ensuring a firm grip on the surface of the soil.

A Cheetah at full speed - notice how the back is arched.

THE FUNCTION OF HOOFS

In *Artiodactyls* (even-toed animals), the extremities of the third and the fourth digits are each covered with a horny hoof to form the cloven hoof. The cloven hoof is important in the mobility of animals in that it allows them to explore a large variety of habitats. In the *Perissodactyls* (odd-toed animals), only the zebra has hoofs. They have retained only the third digit, which is covered in a single hoof.

Depending on the habitat, herbivore hoofs have developed different shapes. The one extreme is the klipspringer, which has stilt-like hoofs with a rubbery consistency, enabling them to jump around on rocks. The other extreme is the sitatunga, a secretive antelope that occurs in swampy areas and has elongated (up to 18 cm long) and pronouncedly splayed hoofs. This allows it to walk on aquatic vegetation to reach papyrus and the other water plants on which it feeds. Lechwes, which utilise the floodplain, also have rather elongated and splayed hoofs to negotiate the mud.

Zebras, with their single-toed hoofs, find it more difficult to transverse soggy areas than the wildebeest and are usually the first to migrate, before the onset of the rains. Impalas, with their small hoofs, only venture onto wet ground when they go to drink water. In all grazers the front hoofs are larger than the back ones since the fore legs take the weight of the body when an animal is grazing.

The 'stiletto' hoof of a klipspringer.

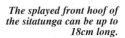

The splayed front hoof of the sitatunga can be up to 18cm long.

THE DIFFERENCE BETWEEN LIGAMENTS AND TENDONS

Ligaments Ligaments function passively and their main purpose is to bind the skeleton together. They also limit the motion of joints. In other words elbows, knees, digits and hocks are prevented from collapsing and bending backwards. One of their most important functions is their antigravity mechanism (see paragraph on hypertrophied nuchal ligament below). Ungulates also have a suspensory mechanism that cushions their footfalls (see 'Springing ligament' below). The claws of cats are passively retracted by elastic ligaments. The suspensorium in the larynx of a lion and leopard is also a ligament (see pg 12 for details).

Tendons Tendons, in contrast to ligaments, function only when muscles function. They transmit the pull of muscles to bones. They are very resistant to tension and very flexible, consisting of parallel bundles of collagenous fibres. The contraction of a large muscle is concentrated by its tendon on a small area of the skeleton. Ligaments function passively and are superior where constant tension is required, such as holding up a heavy head. The significance of tendons is best illustrated in birds. When a bird perches, a toe-locking mechanism is activated by means of the perching tendon, which prevents it from falling off its perch when asleep (Hickman, 1974). As the leg bends, the toes lock. The same mechanism causes the talons of a bird of prey to sink into its victim - as the legs bend under the impact of the strike, the toes lock automatically.

The perchig tendon of a bird (Hickman, 1974).

SPRINGING LIGAMENT

Medium to large animals have evolved ways to save energy when running, through a form of elastic potential energy. This is similar to the elastic potential energy in a drawn archer's bow - in this case, in the stretched ligament. When an ungulate runs and the foot strikes the ground, the impact bends the leg at the fetlock joint (between the phalanges and the cannon bone) which causes the ligament to stretch. This ligament is commonly known as the 'springing ligament'. Ungulates have a sling mechanism that prevents the fetlock joint from collapsing. The sling is attached to the top part of the cannon bone, from which it goes down under the fetlock joint where it is anchored to small bones called sesamoid bones. From there, it splits to anchor just above the hoof, forming a 'swing'. This joint is always bent when weight is exerted on it (in the normal standing position). With impact, the ligament stretches, allowing the joint to bend sharply. As the weight is unloaded, the ligament recovers because of its elasticity and straightens the joint without any muscular effort. This gives an upward impetus to the whole body and the energy saving can be as much as 40%. The major springing ligament of a horse is extremely strong, requiring ± 700kg to break (Hildebrand, 1988).

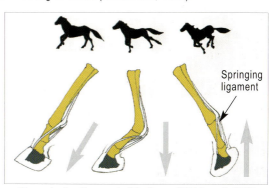

The springing ligament of the horse (Hildebrand, 1988)

HYPERTROPHIED NUCHAL LIGAMENT

All animals with long necks and heavy heads, such as the buffalo and zebra, need to hold their head in a normal, resting position without any muscular effort. This is facilitated by the hypertrophied nuchal ligament which stretches from the occipital crest to the first thoracic vertebra. It is an antigravity mechanism. The head is lowered by a small muscular tug that stretches the ligament and when the muscles relax, the ligament shortens to elevate the head without muscular strain. Elongated spines of the thoracic vertebrae is therefore often associated with a heavy head. This is well illustrated in the equids and the rhinoceros.

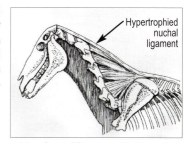

Muscles and ligaments that keep the head up (Hildebrand, 1988).

S K U L L

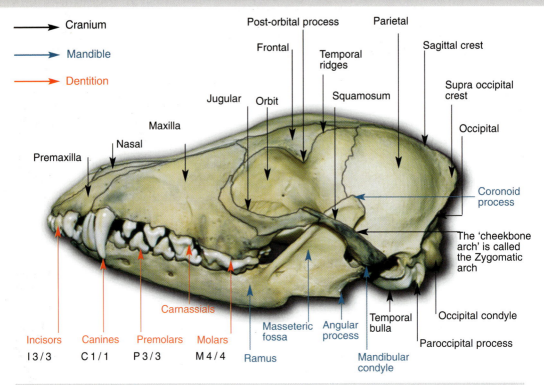

Cranium
Mandible
Dentition

Post-orbital process
Parietal
Frontal
Temporal ridges
Sagittal crest
Supra occipital crest
Jugular
Orbit
Squamosum
Occipital
Maxilla
Nasal
Premaxilla
Coronoid process
The 'cheekbone arch' is called the Zygomatic arch
Carnassials
Incisors
Canines
Premolars
Molars
I 3 / 3
C 1 / 1
P 3 / 3
M 4 / 4
Masseteric fossa
Angular process
Temporal bulla
Occipital condyle
Paroccipital process
Ramus
Mandibular condyle
Temporal bulla

The skull The skull of an animal discloses much about its feeding behaviour - whether it eats meat, grass, leaves, or insects. To enable the reader to understand the structure of the skull, it is necessary to know the names of the different components, for which there are, unfortunately, no 'common' names available. A skull consists of two parts, the **cranium** (which encloses the brain and nasal passages) and the lower jaw or **mandible**. The different skull components are separated from each other by faint cracks or sutures. Remember that 'dorsal means 'on top', 'ventral' means 'underneath', 'lateral' means 'from the side', 'anterior' means 'to the front' and 'posterior' means 'to the back'. Also keep in mind that 'process' refers to a projection and 'foramen' or 'fossa' refers to an opening.

CRANIUM

Dorsal view The dorsal (top) part of the cranium consists of a series of paired bones that meet in the middle. From the front (anterior section) it starts with the **premaxilla** (which holds the top front teeth or incisors), the nasal (which covers the nasal passage), the **maxilla** that holds the premolars and molars and the **frontal** (which extends into the eye-socket or orbit to form the inner wall of the orbit). The **postorbital process** is a projection of the frontal that marks the posterior margin of the eye socket. In some animals it is complete and known as the **postorbital bar**. The **temporal ridges** are near the postorbital process on the frontal and converge further back to form the **sagittal crest**. These ridges are important for muscle attachment to facilitate the movement of the jaw. The sagittal crest in carnivores is enlarged for the attachment of the temporalis muscle, which provides power to the jaw. Herbivores do not need the strength and therefore lack the sagittal crest. The jugular forms the anterior part and the squamosum the posterior part of the zygomatic arch (cheekbones).

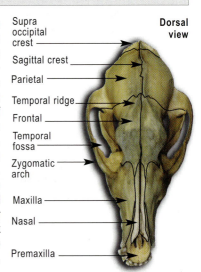

Supra occipital crest
Sagittal crest
Parietal
Temporal ridge
Frontal
Temporal fossa
Zygomatic arch
Maxilla
Nasal
Premaxilla
Dorsal view

Ventral view Underneath, at the base of the zygomatic arch, is the articulation point for the lower jaw - the **mandibular fossa**. In the case of carnivores, which require extreme jaw power, the mandibular fossa forms a groove into which the mandibular condyle fits perfectly. Antelopes and other animals that do not need jaw power, lack the groove. In fact, free movement is essential to permit sideways chewing of tough plant material. Between the occipital condyles and the mandibular fossae are the dome-shaped **auditory / tympanic bullae**, which house the middle and inner ears and which are in direct contact with the brain case. The opening on the side of the bulla is the external **auditory meatus** across which the eardrum is stretched.

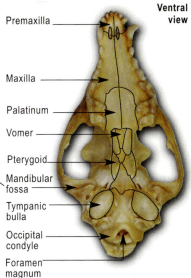

Ventral view

- Premaxilla
- Maxilla
- Palatinum
- Vomer
- Pterygoid
- Mandibular fossa
- Tympanic bulla
- Occipital condyle
- Foramen magnum

The anterior section starts with the **pre-maxilla**, followed by the **maxilla** and then the **palatine bones**, which form the hard palate. The hard palate separates the mouth from the nasal passages. Posterior to the palatine bones and in the middle is a single bone known as the **vomer**, which extends dorsally (upwards) to form the septum between the two nasal passages. Posterior to the palatine bones are the **pterygoid bones**.

Lateral view (Refer to skull on pg 9). Viewed from the side, the **maxilla,** which bears the canines and molars, makes up the largest portion of the front part of the cranium. The conspicuous arch that forms the lower margin of the eye socket and extends posterior to the eye, is called the **zygomatic arch**. It consists of the jugular (anterior) and the squamosum (posterior). The large opening within the zygomatic arch is called the **temporal fossa**, through which some of the muscles of the mandible pass.

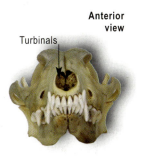

Anterior view

- Turbinals

Anterior view From the front one sees mainly the premaxilla, which holds the incisors, the part of the maxillae that hold the canines and the nasal passage. The highly convoluted or scroll-shaped bones within these passages are called the **turbinals**. The nasal epithelium, which is covered in mucous cells, is folded over these bones to increase the area sensitive to smell.
.

Posterior view Right at the back is the **occipital** and near its centre is the opening that leads the spinal cord into the brain - the **foramen magnum**. The occipital is flanked by two knobs, the **occipital condyles**, which articulate with the first neck vertebra called the atlas. In anatomy the atlas supports the head, just like Atlas, the Titan in Greek mythology who was forced to support the sky on his shoulders as punishment for rebelling against Zeus. Lateral to the occipital condyles are the **paroccipital processes**. These projections are important for the attachment of the digastric muscle, which closes the lower jaw (see pg 12 for details on skull muscles).

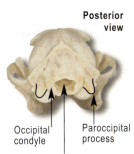

Posterior view

- Occipital condyle
- Paroccipital process
- Foramen magnum

MANDIBLE

The mandible is the lower jaw. The portion in which the teeth are rooted is the **ramus** - the horizontal part of the mandible. The shallow depression on the wide part of the mandible is called the **masseteric fossa** where the masseter muscles attach themselves. At the back there are three projections (in some animals only two are prominent). At the top is the **coronoid process,** which extends into the temporal fossa and provides a surface for the attachment of the temporalis muscle (see pg 12). Below it is the **mandibular condyle**, which articulates with the mandibular fossa of the cranium and forms the point of articulation between cranium and mandible. At the bottom is the **angular process**.

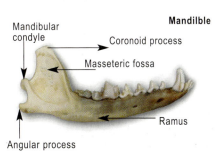

Mandilble

- Mandibular condyle
- Coronoid process
- Masseteric fossa
- Ramus
- Angular process

Ruminants The ruminants all have very similar skulls except for variations in size and horns. They always have post-orbital bars behind the eyes and their skulls are all elongated in the nasal area to form the diastema, the space between the cheekteeth and the incisors, to accommodate a long tongue. They lack incisors and canines in the upper jaw. A wider mandible provides a larger attachment surface for the masseter muscle. This muscle is important for animals that need to masticate their food. Since grasses are tougher than leaves, the mandible is wider in grazers than in browsers. The point of articulation between the cranium and mandible is above the toothrow because jaw power is unnecessary.

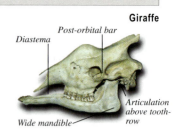

Giraffe

Post-orbital bar
Diastema
Articulation above tooth-row
Wide mandible

Carnivores The temporal muscle of carnivores supplies more than half of the pulling force and enables them to tear raw meat apart. The coronoid process provides the lever arm of this muscle and is therefore very large in carnivores. The point of articulation is nearly in line with the tooth row, providing more power. The mandibular foramen is a transverse groove which limits sideways movement of the lower jaw and adds to the strength of the bite.

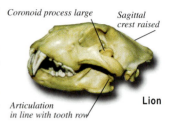

Coronoid process large
Sagittal crest raised

Lion

Articulation in line with tooth row

Animals with heavy heads The area at the back of the skull is known as the nuchal crest or occipital. It is very prominent in animals with large, heavy heads such as the rhino, hippo, elephant and warthog. This provides the surface for the attachment of muscles to hold the heavy head in place. The long spines of the thoracic vertebrae offer attachment for these muscles and ligaments to keep the head up.

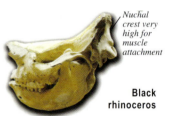

Nuchal crest very high for muscle attachment

Black rhinoceros

Rodents and hares Animals that nibble (hares and rodents) do not need to open their mouths very wide. The point of articulation of the jaw in this group is high above the tooth row. The coronoid process is absent as they do not need much power for nibbling. So, the high part of the mandible is in fact the mandibular condyle (the point of articulation with the cranium). They have a large diastema.

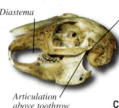

Diastema
Mandibular condyle highest point of mandible, coronoid process absent

Articulation above toothrow

Cape hare

Elephants As a result of the heavy head, a very high occipital crest has evolved to provide sufficient area for muscle attachment. If the skull had evolved as a hollow cranium, it would not be strong enough to withstand forces exerted when pushing over trees and fighting. If it evolved as solid bone, it would be too heavy. The compromise was the formation of toughly constructed 'honeycomb' air cells in the diploe, which provide strength, lightness and resilience. Their orientation and design is such that they can withstand all manner of forces. They only start to form after birth. The head weighs ±17,1% of its total weight (Eltringham, 1991). For a 5 000kg elephant the head will thus weigh ±850kg (a whole buffalo weighs ±820kg). The premaxilla and maxilla form the bone casement that supports the tusks of the elephant. It is not possible to distinguish the different components on the skull of an elephant as all the crack lines are fused.

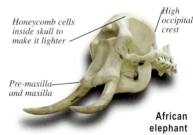

High occipital crest
Honeycomb cells inside skull to make it lighter
Pre-maxilla and maxilla

African elephant

Hippopotamus The eye sockets and nasal area are raised, allowing the hippo to see and breathe while submerged. Articulation of the skull on the axis is specialised, as the entire head can jack-knife upwards, even though the normal resting position is at a strong downward angle. The articulation and the digastric muscle is also specialised. By severe contraction, the digastric is capable of opening the lower jaw to an angle of up to 150°. The mandible is enlarged for attachment of the masseter muscle.

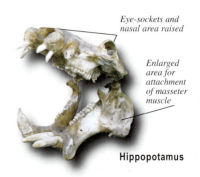

Eye-sockets and nasal area raised
Enlarged area for attachment of masseter muscle

Hippopotamus

Masseter muscle It stretches from the zygomatic arch to the outside of the ramus and its function is to stabilise the articulation of the lower jaw. In simpler terms, it is the muscle that stretches (on the human face) from the cheekbone to the angular part of the jaw. If the area on the lower mandible where the masseter muscle attaches is enlarged, it means that the masseter muscle will have more power. This is important for true grazers that need to masticate tough grasses. An enlarged masseter muscle and high-crowned teeth usually go together. Compare the skull of a browser such as the kudu (narrow with a slim lower jaw) with that of a true grazer - the zebra or the waterbuck - where the lower jaw is deeper, to allow for better muscle attachment.

Temporalis muscle It stretches from the top of the braincase to the coronoid process. In carnivores especially, there is a raised crest above the braincase, called the sagittal crest. It offers an enlarged attachment area for the temporalis muscle. The muscle stretches to the coronoid process, the top of the three projections on the lower jaw. The function of the temporalis muscle is to close the jaw and especially to provide power to the jaw. This muscle is very prominent in carnivores, as is the sagittal crest and coronoid process, especially so in hyaenas that need the strength to crush bones.

Pterogoid muscle It was not possible to indicate this muscle on the illustration, as it is situated on the inside, but just imagine a muscle stretching

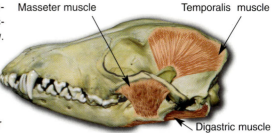

Masseter muscle Temporalis muscle

Digastric muscle

from the vicinity of the throat region of the cranium, to the inside of the lower jaw. It originates at the base of the skull, behind the orbit and beside the palate where it is attached to the pterygoid bones and stretches to the inside of the ramus of the lower jaw. Its function is to close the jaw. This muscle is important for sideways movement of the jaw and is therefore especially important in ungulates that need to mill their food. In carnivores it has the function of positioning the carnassials.

Digastric muscle It stretches from the paroccipital processes to the underside of the mandible and its function is to open the jaw. To remind the reader, the paroccipital processes are situated on the cranium, on the outsides of the occipital condyles (the two bones both sides for the foramen magnum where the spinal chord enters the brain). This muscle is particularly big in animals with a heavy lower jaw. In the case of the hippopotamus, it is specialised to open the jaw at an unusual angle of up to 150°, which is done during aggressive displays.

THE SKULL BONES WE DO NOT SEE

Hyoid apparatus The series of small bones that support the tongue and suspend the larynx from the base of the skull is called the hyoid apparatus. It forms a kind of suspended 'swing', starting from just behind the ear bulla on the one side, through the base of the tongue, to behind the ear bulla on the other side. The middle section of the bones is attached to the larynx. In the genus *Panthera* (lions and leopards) this middle section is modified to become an elastic ligament known as the **suspensorium**. Elasticity of the hyoid apparatus allows for a large cavity to form when air is forced through it, which acts as an amplification 'box'. This enables lions and leopards to utter a load roar. They are the only cats that can roar and the enlarged amplification area explains why a lion's roar 'makes the earth tremble' and why a

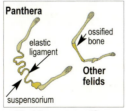

Panthera

ossified bone

elastic ligament

Other felids

suspensorium

Hyoid apparatus (from Skinner & Smithers, 1990)

leopard's 'saw' can be heard over such a long distance. The other cats (subfamily *Felis*) as well as the cheetah, are called the purring cats. They produce the typical purring sound that we know from domestic cats. The purr is produced when air is forced over the hardened bone of the hyoid apparatus. Interestingly, lions and leopards can also purr but it is limited to exhalation. As we know with domestic cats, they purr both with inhalation and exhalation and it usually signifies contentment.

The ear-bones The other bones we do not see are the smallest bones in the body - the minute bones within the ear bullae - the stapes, incus and malleus. The stapes (stirrup) in humans measures only 2,6-3,4mm. Read more on pg 17 and 18.

D E N T I T I O N

DENTAL STRUCTURES AND FORMULAS

Dental structures *Herbivores:* Dental structures of grazers and browsers differ considerably. Grazers have to cope with very fibrous material whereas browsers eat mainly leaves that are less fibrous and tough. Grazers have finely textured surfaces on high-crowned molars to mill the tough grass stems while browsers have more prominent cusps for cutting twigs and leaves. The high-crowned teeth of grazers are essential because of the presence of silica in the grass - a tough substance which wears normal teeth easily. Such high-crowned teeth are called 'hypsodont' dental structures. *Carnivores:* Carnivore teeth are adapted for killing. The canines are enlarged and long and the molars are adapted for slicing.

Dental formula The lower and upper teeth in the front of the mouth are called incisors (I),

followedby the canines (C). The cheekteeth are represented by pre-molars (P) to the front of the mouth and the true molars (M) at the back. The numbers are expressed in a simple dental formula to show one half of both jaws. The numbers left of the line represent the upper jaw and the ones on the right of the line the lower jaw. The formula for the skull below will thus be I3/3 C1/1 P3/3 M4/4 = 44. To calculate the total number of teeth the sum of the formula is multiplied by 2: 3+3+1+1+3+3+4+4 = 22 x 2 = 44.

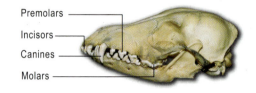

Premolars

Incisors

Canines

Molars

DENTITION OF DIFFERENT GROUPS

Ruminant Ruminants have such an extensively specialised digestive system (see pg 22), that the teeth are secondary. The lower jaw retains its incisors and canines, the latter often taking on the shape of the incisors. The incisors as well as the canines are absent from the upper jaw and what remains is a horny pad against which the lower incisors press when biting. The significance of the relatively soft pad is to reduce wear of the lower incisors to the minimum. The teeth of grazers do eventually wear off in old age, to the point where there is no crown left. The premolars and molars are present in both the top and bottom jaws. The tongues of all antelopes are long and prehensile for the selection of food. To make space for the tongue, the jaw is elongated and the resulting toothless space between the incisors and the molars, is called the diastema.

Only lower incisors

Diastema

Common duiker

Rhinoceros They lack canine and incisor teeth in both jaws, but the broad lips of the white rhino are perfectly suited to pluck grass, and the pointed upper lip of the black rhino is ideal for gathering grass. The molars and pre-molars of the white rhino, which is a grazer, are particularly high-crowned with fine surfaces - well adapted for masticating the grass.

Only premolars and molars

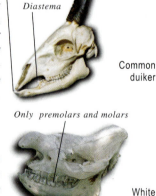

White rhinoceros

Zebra The zebra has a single stomach and has to rely more on grinding the food properly before swallowing. Therefore the teeth are long (hypsodont) to accommodate the wear. In fact, they grow longer with age, explaining the saying 'long in the tooth'. Zebras have retained both sets of incisors, enabling them to nip off the grass stems. Their digestive system is well adapted to make use of the sugar in the grass stems.

Upper and lower incisors

Zebra

Warthog Warthogs have elongated, curved canines which are firmly encased in bony sockets. They are used for self defence and rooting. Lower canines occlude against upper ones and are razor sharp. The incisor teeth do not serve much purpose as they have minimum occlusion, are rounded and forward sloping. They use their lips to nip off the grass.

Canines used for rooting and fighting

Warthog

Elephant The upper incisor teeth have been transformed into tusks. There are six molars that are periodically replaced during the elephant's lifetime at roughly the following ages: M1 - birth to 1 year; M2 - 2 years; M3 - 6 years; M4 - 15 years; M5 - 28 years; M6 - 47 years. They are replaced from the back and the old molars are pushed out in front. The mandible is very short and heavy, and 'hangs' from the temporalis muscle like the chair of a swing. The temporalis muscle inserts (attaches) on the side and top of the cranium and attaches to the coronoid process. The entire lower jaw can slide freely to and fro over the curved squamosal of the cranium. This accommodates the elephant's manner of grinding - from back to front, and not sideways.

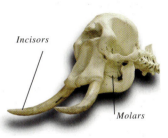

Incisors

Molars

African
elephant

Hippopotamus Hippos retain their incisor and canine teeth in both jaws, but these are used only for fighting and self-defence, not for feeding. The molars are high-crowned to accommodate wear caused by tough grasses. The wide, flattened, hard lips are used very effectively to pluck the grass.

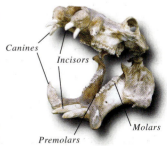

Canines

Incisors

Molars

Premolars

Hippopotamus

Carnivores The carnivores retain upper and lower incisors, canines, premolars and molars. In most species the canines are very well developed and elongated for killing their prey effectively. Most species in this group also have carnassials. This is where the fourth upper premolar and the first lower molar occlude in such a way that they form blade-like edges, enabling the carnivore to cut through the toughest skin and bones. In species that do not eat exclusively meat, like civets, the molars are better suited for crushing (broad and flat) than for shearing.

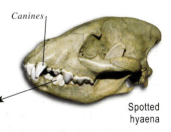

Canines

Spotted
hyaena

The power of the slicing carnassials is further enhanced by a hinge-joint of the mandible and the cranium, preventing any movement of the jaws. This adds tremendous stability and enables the animal to hold on to its prey. Cats have shorter skulls with a reduced number of cheekteeth.

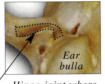

*Ear
bulla*

*Hinge-joint where
mandible fits in
tightly*

Carnassials

Pangolin

Aardvark
teeth

Aardwolf

Pangolin

Aardvark

Aardwolf The molars of the aardwolf are reduced to pegs. They feed on termites and do not need to grind their food.

Pangolin It has no teeth at all, as its stomach does the work of teeth, functioning like a bird's gizzard

Aardvark The teeth consist of densely packed, 6-sided tubules surrounded by dentine. Their teeth lack enamel.

Incisors

Rock
hyrax

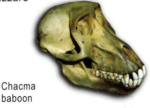

Chacma
baboon

Incisors

Bush
squirrel

Hyrax The hyrax has two ever-growing incisor teeth, almost like the tusks of an elephant.

Primates They have teeth for an omnivorous diet, like humans, but also have large incisors for self-defence and for occasionally killing small vertebrates.

Rodents They have ever-growing, gnawing incisors that occlude against each other to keep them sharp. They lack canines and have a large diastema (toothless area).

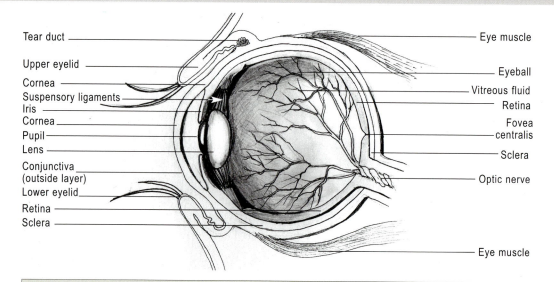

Tear duct — Eye muscle
Upper eyelid — Eyeball
Cornea — Vitreous fluid
Suspensory ligaments — Retina
Iris
Cornea — Fovea centralis
Pupil
Lens — Sclera
Conjunctiva (outside layer) — Optic nerve
Lower eyelid
Retina
Sclera

Eye muscle

ANATOMY OF THE EYE

Structure of the eye All animals have superior vision but before one can understand why, one has to understand the structure of the eye and how it works.

The edges of the lids are folds in the skin and the skin actually continues over and behind the eye. The epidermis becomes the conjunctiva, which covers the front of the eye, and the dermis becomes the sclera at the back and the cornea in front.

Imagine the eye to be a spherical ball covered in various layers, of which the conjunctiva forms the outer layer. Inside that is the dermis (cornea in front and sclera at the back). The inner layer consists of the retina and the core consists of vitreous fluid.

The light that enters the eye has to be controlled and this is done by a 'curtain' or the iris (the coloured part of the eye). This 'curtain' surrounds the light window or the pupil. The pupil is lined by a non-reflective black pigment to reduce random reflection of light within the eye. When light is dim, the 'curtain' pulls back and the pupil enlarges. When it is bright, the 'curtain' closes and the pupil becomes small. The iris is controlled by tiny muscles.

Rod cells and cone cells The light enters through the pupil, goes through the lens that is behind it and through the vitreous core to the light-sensitive cells that are situated on the retina, more or less at the back of the spherical eyeball. The photoreceptor cells in the retina consist of rod cells that are long and slender, and of cone cells that are conical in shape. The rod cells respond to a single quantum of light energy but the cones, which have different pigments, respond to light of different wavelengths. Cone cells are thus responsible for colour vision. Rods are about four times more sensitive than cones but they do not record colour. Strictly nocturnal animals have only rod cells and they perceive the world in black, white and grey. Contrary to popular belief, animals are not all colour blind. Dogs, horses and sheep can all distinguish colour, although not as well as humans. Primates, especially chimpanzees and the rhesus monkey, have colour vision that is equal or almost equal to man.

How the 'area centralis' provides sharp vision The sharpest image is perceived in an area called the *area centralis*, or *fovea centralis*, which is situated in a direct line with the centre of the lens and the cornea. It contains only cone cells, which are very compact. Good vision depends on how many nerve cells there are in this area. Humans and lions have about the same number of cones - ±125 000 - 150 000 cones / mm^2, but birds of prey may have up to 1,5 million / mm^2 (Hickman, 1974). In many animals, but more especially in birds of prey, the fovea forms a pit. It has the function of bending the light rays to enlarge the image - up to as much as 30% in some cases (read more about vision in birds of prey on pg 16).

Why do eyes reflect at night?

The eyes of most mammals reflect light because of a 'mirror' of reflective crystals situated at the back of the eyes behind the rod cells. This mirror is called the '*tapetum lucidum*'. The 'reflective crystals' cause the light to travel twice through the rods, increasing the chance of triggering a nerve impulse, providing the animals with excellent night vision. A lion, for instance, can see in light that is only one sixth as bright as that which is needed by humans.

Most felines (cats) have poorly developed colour vision, which means they see the world in black, white and grey. The crystalline layer enables them to absorb 50% more light than the human eye. That explains why, during the day, the cat's irises contract into slits to screen out the bright light. At night, however, they are round to let in the maximum amount of light.

Binocular vision

Many birds, such as sandpipers, have eyes set on each side of the head, with each eye seeing a different scene. Although they have a wide field of vision their binocular vision (to judge distance) is almost non-existent. Sandpipers compensate for this lack of stereoscopic vision by bobbing their heads up and down and sideways to view an object from several angles. Herons, on the other hand,

Side and 'rear' vision good — Binocular vision limited

Zebras and other ungulates have a wide field for vision but relatively limited binocular vision.

Side and 'rear' vision limited

Binocular vision good

Lions have much better binocular vision as their eyes are situated to the front of the skull.

which take on a 'freezing stance' when hunting, have excellent binocular vision.

Horizontal pupil

All ungulates have exceptional eyesight. Antelopes have a horizontal pupil, enabling them to see more or less behind them from the outside corner of the eye. This is aided by the fact that the eyes are situated on the sides of the head. Unfortunately, this has an adverse affect on their binocular vision, which means that they don't judge distances very well. Therefore, animals that need an acute depth perception to hunt or to climb trees and jump from branch to branch, have forward-looking eyes, the best examples being cats and primates. In this regard the klipspringer, a small rock-dwelling antelope, is an exception among antelopes. The klipspringer's eyes are set forward in the skull to enable them to judge distances when leaping from rock to rock.

Nictitating membrane

This is the third eyelid or 'haw' and is quite prominent in birds and reptiles. It moves across the eyeball from the inside to the outside and has the function of cleaning the eye and to protect it. It also occurs in certain mammals, especially in predators that need protection during the dangers of hunting. Otters have transparent membranes that allow them to see under water.

THE SUPERIOR VISION OF BIRDS OF PREY

Birds of prey have exceptional eyesight, keener than all animals and far superior to humans. They have large eyes, a high concentration of nerve cells and highly developed eye muscles. In the light-sensitive retina there is a foveal pit containing light-sensitive cone cells. A buzzard, for example, has about one million of these cones per mm², as opposed to ±125 000 in man. That makes their eyes as good as human eyes would be if aided by eight-power binoculars. They also have built-in telescopic vision. As the light rays strike the pit, they are bent outward, thus magnifying the image by as much as 30%. They are said to be able to see a crouching hare

Hawks have two foveal pits.

at ±1,6km or one mile (Hickman, 1974). Hawks have two fovea in each eye, one directed forward to enhance binocular vision and the other to the sides, to enhance monocular vision (see illustration). They can thus focus on more than one object at the same time. Falcons often catch their prey in the air at speeds of up to 200km/h. To enable them to keep their prey in sharp focus, their eye muscles are extremely well developed to control the curvature of the lens and adjust the focal length. The eyes of owls are extremely sensitive to light and they can see in light from one-tenth to up to one-hundredth the intensity required by humans (Hickman, 1974).

ANATOMY OF THE EAR

To appreciate the acute hearing of wild mammals, it is necessary to understand the structure of the ear. The bone-covered domes situated on the ventral side of the cranium, known as the auditory bullae, house the inner and middle ears (refer to section on 'dorsal view' of the skull on pg 9). The opening to the side of each bullae is the external auditory meatus across which the eardrum or tympanic membrane is stretched. This membrane is surrounded by a small circular bone known as the tympanic bone. The bullae are attached to and associated with the brain-case. The ear consists of three parts:

The outer ear It consists of the skin-covered flap or pinna and the auditory canal. In most animals the pinnae are freely movable like radar receptors that collect sound waves. The auditory canal, which leads to the eardrum, condenses the sound waves and passes them to the tympanic membrane or eardrum.

The middle ear In all other vertebrates the lower jaw consists of several bones, but in mammals it consists of a single bone. Some of the bones of more primitive vertebrates have been converted to form two of the three little bones (ossicles) in the middle ear as well as the tympanic bone, which surrounds the eardrum. The middle ear is air-filled, with a chain of three tiny bones, the malleus (hammer), the incus (anvil) and the stapes (stirrup). This bridge of bones carries the sound on to the inner ear by means of the stirrup, which hits against the oval window - a membrane or 'drum' with a smaller area, having the effect of

magnifying the sound. The overall result is an amplification of about 90 times. These three bones are the smallest in the mammal body and in humans the stapes (stirrup) measures only 2,6-3,4mm. The cochlea has a spiralled shape like a sea shell. It makes about 2,5 turns in man and as many as five turns in animals, providing them with more nerve cells and better hearing. High frequencies are sensed at the base of the cochlea and low frequencies towards the tip. Very loud sounds are dampened by the contraction of muscles attached to the middle ear bones, but they do not react fast enough to dampen a gun shot or a blast. The nerve cells in the cochlea can be damaged by high noise levels and may even die, resulting in partial deafness. This is why ear mufflers are a requirement at a shooting range.

The inner ear The inner ear consists of the hearing organ (the cochlea) and the organ of balance (the semi-circular canals). The part involved with transmitting the soundwaves to the brain is situated in the cochlea, a structure that consists of three fluid-filled ducts which lengthen and coil to form the cochlea or 'snail shell'.

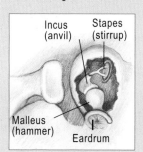

The middle ear.

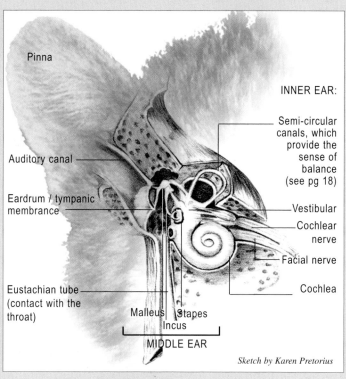

Pinna

Auditory canal

Eardrum / tympanic membrane

Eustachian tube (contact with the throat)

Incus (anvil) Stapes (stirrup)

Malleus (hammer) Eardrum

Malleus Stapes Incus

MIDDLE EAR

INNER EAR:

Semi-circular canals, which provide the sense of balance (see pg 18)

Vestibular

Cochlear nerve

Facial nerve

Cochlea

Sketch by Karen Pretorius

The outer, middle and inner ear of the mammal.

The best way to understand how the sound waves are transmitted is to imagine stretching out the cochlea into a straight tube. The three canals will be distinguished as the vestibular canal at the top, the tympanic canal at the bottom and the cochlear canal in the middle. So, when the stirrup hits the oval window, it creates waves in the fluid in the top canal (vestibular canal) which turns sharply on itself into a parallel tube, the tympanic canal. Between the two is the cochlear duct, which houses a layer of hair cells containing the organ of hearing - the organ of corti. As the hair cells are stimulated, the organ of corti transmits the information to the brain by means of nerve cells. The brain then interprets these as tones.

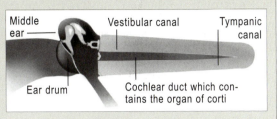

The 'stretched out' cochlea to illustrate how sound is transmitted to the brain.

INTERESTING FACTS ABOUT HEARING

Noise levels in decibels Noise levels are measured in decibels (dB). The level of just audible sound is taken at 0dB, and a jet aircraft emits about 140dB. Listening to music by means of earphones can easily pass the 100 decibel mark and because it is so close to the ear, this can permanently damage the sensitive cells in the cochlea. Interesting to note is that blue whales have been recorded emitting sounds of 188 decibels - much louder than a jet plane. The sounds are not within human range. However, it was found that with sound equipment it was possible to pick up the whale calls over a 3 000km stretch!

Blocked ears The eustachian tube connects the middle ear cavity with the throat, preventing the pressure in the middle ear cavity from becoming so high that it ruptures the ear drum. That is the familiar 'blocked ears' that one experiences when ascending or descending in an aircraft. The lower end of the tube closes up when the pressure increases and can be rectified, at least partially, by swallowing.

Range of hearing The range of human hearing is between 20Hz and 20 000Hz (Hz signifies one vibration per second). All mammals have better hearing than man, cats being able to hear frequencies of 78 000Hz, dogs up to 30 000Hz or 40 000Hz and bats up to 230 000Hz. It is of interest to mention here that dogs can hear many of the sounds emitted by vampire bats, and are therefore not attacked by them. The reason is because vampire bats, that prey on large mammals, do not emit such high frequencies as insect-eating bats, making their calls audible to dogs. The insect-eating bats like the horseshoe bats have folds on their faces that have the double function of channelling the sound in a narrow beam so that it can transmit further, and of directing the received impulses to the ears. Many of the low, rumbling sounds made by elephants (which are made by the larynx, not the stomach), are also not audible to the human ear as they are lower than 20Hz infra sound. Elephants are said to be able to hear sounds as low as 12Hz (Hildebrand, 1988), or even lower.

Echolocation in bats Read more about it on pg 115.

External ears The external ears of all grazers are mobile and their funnel shape is ideal to direct sound to the eardrum. While they are grazing in a vulnerable position with their heads down, the ears work like radar receptors, informing them about approaching danger.

Aquatic mammals Aquatic mammals receive sound at very high frequencies by means of echolocation. Dolphins detect ultrasound frequencies of ±150 000Hz. Dolphins have no vocal chords but they communicate by forcing air past flaps located below the blowhole. They hunt by using echo-location in much the same way bats do. Whales communicate in the same way, but as was indicated earlier, the sounds they emit can be extremely load and carry very far (see paragraph one).

Sense of balance Closely connected to the inner ear are three semicircular canals. They are filled with fluid and are orientated in each plane of space at right angles to each other. At the opening of each is a bulb-like enlargement, called the ampulla, which contains hair cells. When the fluid moves, the hair cells are stimulated, which in turn sends messages to the brain and produces consciousness of movement and orientation. It is very well developed in cats.

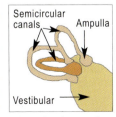

Semicircular canals.

S E N S E   O F   S M E L L

ANATOMY OF THE NASAL CHAMBER

In mammals the surface area of the nasal chamber is increased by the turbinates. The turbinates are scroll-shaped bones which are folded into the nasal chamber from the lateral bones. These bones can clearly be seen on skulls within the nasal cavity. The nasal epithelium, which is covered in mucous cells, is folded over

The 'scroll bones' of the lion.

these bones to increase the area sensitive to smell. The sense of smell is a chemical sense, in which chemical particles are dissolved on the mucous membrane. The primary function of the folded epithelium is to clean and moisten inspired air, while also increasing the chances of detecting a smell because of the larger surface. The olfactory cells continue as axons into the olfactory bulb of the brain. Herbivores have a fair sense of smell, which they use mainly to detect predators and to determine the palatability of plant species. For example, they are deterred by grasses with a strong smell like Turpentine grass (*Cymbopogon*

excavatus). Herbivores also have the ability to smell water from very far away. In animals where smell is vital for obtaining food, the olfactory bulbs are enlarged. In this regard the aardvark is an excellent example as it relies almost completely on its sense of smell to detect its subterranian food source - termites. The olfactory bulbs in the brain of the aardvark are exceptionally large. Canids also have an acute sense of smell, which is evident in their elongated nasal area, more so than felines, which already have an above average sense of smell. The elephant's sense of smell is much better than even that of a dog. Elephant trainers believe that elephants can be trained to locate landmines by means of smell. The sense of smell is aided in most animals by the vomero-nasal organ or Jacobson's organ, which is situated in the roof of the mouth (read more on pg 20).

R E P R O D U C T I O N

Introduction Reproduction is one of the strongest instincts in mammals, maybe only surpassed by the instinct to eat. Everything concerned with reproduction is 'orchestrated' in an epicentre of the brain called the hypothalamus. It is situated just below the brain and just above the pituitary gland. The latter is responsible for releasing hormones into the system to control reproduction, but only after getting the 'instructions' from the hypothalamus. Before we get into the biological processes, we need to look at the social boundaries within which each species operates.

Mating systems The social boundaries of mammals can be compared to the human institution of marriage or even the acceptability of polygamy in certain cultures. Animals also have monogamous (one mate) or polygamous (more mates) mating systems and it is roughly summed up in the diagram on pg 20. Do take note that there are variations depending on factors such as climate, food availability and population densities.

Mating cycles Mating depends on when a female is biologically ready to mate, which in turn is governed by mating cycles or estrous cycles. The cycles depend very much on the species but there are three main types: *Mono-estrous:* There is only one cycle per year. *Di-estrous:* There are two cycles per year. *Poly-estrous:* There are many

cycles per year, varying in frequency for each species.

Stimuli that bring on the estrous cycle
Poly-estrous mammals: In poly-estrous animals the cycles recur periodically without any stimulus, like in humans. In the case of lions, estrous occurs about every three weeks and lasts for about one week. *Day length:* Most cycles are determined by day length but there are short-day breeders and long-day breeders. The short-day breeders are most of the antelope, which mate in autumn (when days become short) to ensure that they have their young in spring. They have gestation periods varying from six to eight months. Long-day breeders are usually the mammals with short gestation periods (one to two months). If they mate in the beginning of spring, they can still produce their offspring in summer when food is more plentiful.

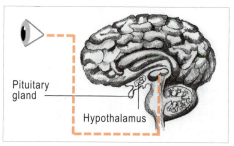

Pituitary gland

Hypothalamus

The brain, hypothalamus and the pituitary gland

MATING SYSTEMS

Monogamy

Mate for life

Jackals, foxes, aardwolf
Bat-eared fox, Cape fox,
Side-striped jackal, Black-
backed jackal, aardwolf

Dwarf antelopes
Grysbok, Suni, Oribi,
Common duiker,
Klipspringer, Steenbok,
Dik-dik, Blue duiker, Red
duiker

Elephant shrews

Only alpha male and female breeds

African wild dog
Dwarf mongoose
Porcupine
Suricates
Molerats

Polygamy

Polygyny (*One male mates with many different females*)

Herd-forming antelopes
Gemsbok, Sable, Roan, Red
hartebeest, Wildebeest,
Tsessebe, Waterbuck, Red
lechwe, Puku, Mountain
reedbuck, Common reed-
buck, Impala

Other group-forming mammals
Hippopotamus
Bushpig
Hyrax
Zebra
Vervet monkey
Warthog

Polyganandry (*Males and females mate with multiple mates*)

Spiral-horned antelope
Eland, Kudu, Bushbuck,
Sitatunga, Nyala

Solitary animals
Aardvark, Leopard, Cheetah,
African wild cat, Black-footed
cat, Caracal, Serval, Civet,
Genets, Striped polecat,
Slender mongoose, Honey
badger, Pangolin, Springhare,
Rhinos, Otters

Social animals
Buffalo, Baboons, Banded
mongoose, Hyaenas,
Elephants

Where day length governs the cycles, the process seems to be as follows: light enters the eye, which stimulates the pineal gland in the brain to decrease its production of melatonin, a chemical that inhibits the growth of the reproductive organs. The animal thus becomes ready to breed. At the same time the hypothalamus stimulates the pituitary gland just beneath the brain to secrete the hormones FSH and LH (FSH = Follicle stimulating hormone and LH = Luteinizing hormone). These stimulate the ovaries in females to start the process of egg-formation and the testes in males to produce testosterone, the latter which will start preparing the male for the rut.

Shellie Roodt

A male lion exhibiting the flehmen grimace

Pheromones and 'flehmen' Most animals rely heavily on pheromones, scent glands and urine to convey olfactory messages to each other regarding their territories or sexual availability. Animals have an extra sense organ hidden in the roof of the mouth, between the hard palate and the nasal cavity. It is called the vomero-nasal organ or Jacobson's organ, which enables them to interpret subtle olfactory messages. The way to access this organ, is to exhibit 'flehmen', which basically means 'urine-tasting'. This is done by both males and females, but mostly by males when a female is in estrous. They lick the urine or genitalia and then exhibit the flehmen grimace in which the upper lip is curled upwards. The grimace is actually necessary to activate certain muscles that will initiate a series of processes and responses. The naso-palatine duct connects the mouth with the vomero-nasal organ by means of a small incisive foramen (opening) in the front part of the palate. The action of the lip-raising muscles, the *musculus levator labii*, exerts an upward and backward force which opens the cartilaginous prongs that keep the opening to the vomero-nasal opening closed. A slight vacuum is formed which sucks in the molecules from the tongue. The vomero-nasal nerve connects with the accessory olfactory bulb, which is situated next to the main olfactory bulb. The main olfactory bulb conveys messages directly from the nasal epithelium to the brain. The accessory olfactory bulb seems to convey more subtle messages. It is connected to the amygdaloid nucleus. This is an association centre for olfactory input and it contributes to arousal, emotions and food intake.

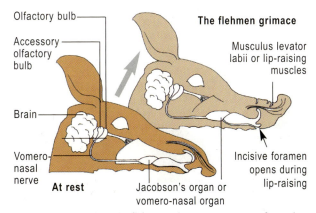

A diagram to show how the flehmen grimace opens up an alternative route for olfactory messages to the brain

The amygdaloid projects to the hypothalamus. Once the molecules have found their way to this epicenter, the biological processes will take their course. As was pointed out earlier, the hypothalamus is the endocrine control centre and lies at the underside of the brain above the

Shellie Roodt
The 'mating game' of a giraffe can go on for days on end

very important pituitary gland. The pituitary gland is responsible for releasing hormones that dictate sexual behaviour and responses as well as growth and other functions. Simple peptides known as releasing hormones are released from the hypothalamus in response to certain stimuli like smells. The pituitary gland then releases hormones (LH and FSH) that control the reproductive process in females and the testosterone levels in males.

The vomero-nasal organ is rudimentary or absent in some primates, aquatic mammals, birds, crocodiles, turtles and humans. There are two exceptions worth mentioning here. The pig relies heavily on scent stimuli but they do not exhibit flehmen behaviour because their lip musculator structure does not allow it. Their lips are adapted for shovelling and therefore they do not have the muscle to 'lip-curl'. The other exception is equids, where flehmen behaviour is most evident, but the canal from the roof of the mouth is blind, therefore all contact is through the nasal cavity (Stoddart,1980).

Delay mechanisms There is usually a time period required to ensure that the best genes are reproduced. It can take the following forms: *Rut*: The goal in reproduction is for the best genes to be reproduced for the ultimate benefit of the species. In most species it is the strongest male that gets the female(s). Even in monogamous pairs the more dominant male is more likely to find a partner. In many cases the males first determine their dominance hierarchy by means of a rut, which is so evident for example in impalas. This is, in a way, a kind of delay mechanism because once the male has secured his dominance and his herd, mating is swift, taking less than a minute per female in many species. In these animals the actual receptive period is very short and therefore the male has to act swiftly. *Spiral-horned antelope:* The spiral-horned antelopes rely much more on physical size, horn size and visual display (strutting) and it is very often the largest male that impregnates the female. Since their system is one of differ-

Shellie Roodt
As with domestic animals, same-sex simulated matings often take place in the wild

ent males visiting the female in heat, a period of delay is necessary to allow enough males to do the rounds. Therefore the receptive period of spiral-horned antelopes is longer than other herd-forming, polygynous antelope. The female only actually ovulate in the last few hours of her estrous. Aggressive fighting is not common in this group. A stance is usually enough to convey the message. *Initial rejection:* It is very common to see females ignoring the attention of a male or trying to get away from him - in simple terms 'playing hard to get'. This may last for days or longer in the case of elephants and giraffe. This is also just a delay mechanism to attract the strongest male. Once the female is ready to mate, she presents herself in a position called 'lordosis'.

Induced ovulation This kind of ovulation usually occurs in animals that are poly-estrous such as cats, hares and rodents. In this case a female needs physical stimulation to induce ovulation and it mostly requires multiple matings, often in short succession, to achieve this. The lion is a very good example, because one often gets the opportunity to observe their mating process. All carnivores, except hyaenas, rodents, insectivores and bats have an *os penis* or baculum, which is a small bone in the penis (see pg 4). There seems to be a correlation between the presence of a baculum and induced ovulation, although the canids do not practise induced ovulation (but they do have a baculum). Another very interesting aspect is that the males of induced ovulators seem to develop spines on the glans (tip of the penis), which seems to have a further stimulating effect to induce ovulation. In the domestic cat, the feature of penile spines are dependent on the production of androgen. *Lions and induced ovulation:* The male lion has barbs on the the glans of the penis that are about 1mm long. This makes the mating mildly painful for the female, often resulting in her breaking away and attacking the male. The scraping effect on the vagina wall stimulates the brain to release a hormone that releases the egg. The sperm cells lodge themselves in the womb's wall until the egg is released. The sperm cells can survive for 24 hours. When the sperm enters the egg, a hard shell is immediately formed, preventing other sperms from entering. The womb of the lioness shows a special adaptation that enables the female to continue hunting while pregnant. There is a hammock-like protection sling around each foetus which helps to absorb the impact of a powerful collision with a prey animal. In relation to other animals of similar size, the uterus wall is also much thicker to absorb the impact (National Geographic). *Monogamous mating system:* In the case of monogamy, a mating partner is guaranteed but the act of mating is often a vulnerable position to be in. Therefore, canids have devised a method that will ensure impregnation with a single or very few matings - quite the opposite of the system in cats. After penetration, the base of the penis swells and at the same time the female vulva also swells, locking them together. To enable them to remain vigilant, the male reverses his position by cocking his leg over the female's back while they are locked so that they both face in different directions. Only when the swelling goes down can the male free himself (Carnaby, 2006). In domestic dogs this 'locking position' may continue for more than an hour.

Delayed reproduction in Bats (see pg 113-118).

DIGESTIVE SYSTEMS

HERBIVORES

THE RUMINANT STOMACH

Ruminants are foregut fermenters and have evolved a superior ability to convert cellulose and fibres to digestible matter by remasticating their food (chewing the cud) and by allowing micro-organisms in the rumen to complete the process. *Mouth:* Digestion begins in the mouth where large quantities of saliva are mixed with the food. The saliva has a digestive enzyme that is responsible for the digestion of starch. The saliva is also responsible for the alkalisation of the food. A high alkalinity is necessary to minimise the possibility of bloat, the latter being caused mainly by a high acid content of the food. A large bovine produces as much as 200 litres of saliva per day during the feeding process - just imagine - a large 200 litre drum full of saliva! The ruminant stomach consists of the following:

Rumen, a roughly s-shaped sac which is the largest of the four stomachs and which is lined with a myriad of tiny finger-like protuberances.
Reticulum 'honeycomb', which is lined with hexagonal ridges.
Omasum, which is sometimes called the prayer-book or leaf stomach because of the page-like structure.
Abomasum, which is similar to the ordinary stomach of a non-ruminant such as a pig or a horse.

Rumen: The ruminant eats as fast as possible and does not waste much time chewing because of its vulnerable position while feeding - head down in the case of grazers. The rumen can be described as a kind of storage organ, which, in the case of grazers, comprises as much as 15-20 % of the total body weight. In large bovines this may amount to a volume of 180 litres. It is in fact much more than a storage organ because apart from storing the food, the rumen contracts rhythmically to mix the food. It also acts as a filter operating on the principle of specific gravity where the smaller food particles sink to the bottom and the larger parts float in the upper layers.

From there the food re-enters the oesophagus and goes back to the mouth for remastication. Millions of minute animal and plant organisms (protozoa, bacteria and yeast cells) exist in the rumen and their main function is to break down tough plant material such as cellulose and lignin - a function that the normal digestive juices are not able to fulfil. When the organisms reach the end of their life, they are absorbed as additional protein. *Reticulum:* This has very much the same function as the rumen and the two are often referred to as the reticulorumen. *Omasum:* It is also known as the 'leaf-stomach' where the food is ground into fine particles. *Abomasum:* It is similar to the stomach of other animals and here digestive juices are added for the first time to complete the process. The food goes into the small intestine from where it is absorbed. The small intestine in some ruminants is extremely long, about 43m in the wildebeest. The abomasum is also called the 'milk-stomach' because when a calf suckles or when an animal drinks water, the liquid goes straight to the abomasum via the oesophageal groove. It is also possible to administer medicine directly to the stomach via the groove by first administering bluestone orally to the animal, which causes the groove to close for a while. Otherwise the chemical composition of the medicine may be altered in the rumen.

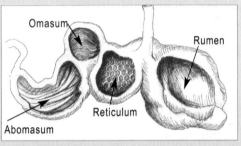

The four chambers in the digestive system of ruminants.

DIFFERENCE BETWEEN FOREGUT AND HINDGUT FERMENTERS

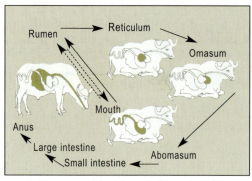

Movement of food through the ruminant's digestive system.

All herbivores can be classified as foregut or hindgut fermenters. In foregut fermenters, fermentation takes place before the food reaches the stomach and in hindgut fermenters it takes place in the caecum, after the food has left the stomach. The human appendix is a vestige of the caecum. Whether a foregut or hindgut fermenter, grazers generally have large fermentation chambers with moderate surface papillation and small openings between stomachs for slower movement of food. Browsers have numerous papillae and large openings for fast movement of food.

FOREGUT FERMENTERS

Hippopotamus Foregut fermenters include all the ruminants and the hippopotamus. Although the latter is not a ruminant, its digestive system can be compared to that of a ruminant as fermentation takes place in the anterior (front) section of its huge stomach. **Ruminants** Refer to box on pg 22.

HINDGUT FERMENTERS

Hindgut fermenters include the warthog, the zebra, the two rhinoceroses and the elephant. In hindgut fermenters, the food goes straight to an enzymatic stomach after which it passes through the small intestine into the caecum. The caecum acts as a fermentation chamber together with the colon. There is no prior digestion of protein by microbes, making protein digestion less effective in this group. The advantage of a hindgut fermenter is that double the amount of food can pass through the digestive tract during the same time period. So, if there is an abundance of low quality food, a zebra will survive on a diet that is too low in protein to support a ruminant. However, if the food is limited, the zebra will die before the ruminant.

CARNIVORES

Carnivores in general Carnivore and scavenger digestion is quite on the other end of the scale compared to herbivores. They eat very nutritious food, high in protein, and they devour it in the shortest period of time possible. They have long intervals inbetween for rest and play. They invest huge amounts of energy in obtaining their food and consequently make sure they reap the benefits. They therefore either cache their food or gorge themselves, preventing others from stealing it. Their digestive physiology and anatomy are well adapted to accommodate this gorging habit. Temporary storage is therefore essential and for this reason they have a remarkably distensible oesophagus. The stomach itself is also distensible. You just have to look at the stomach of a lion, especially the dominant male, at a kill. The males eat first and make sure they get their fill before they share. That 'fill' may amount to 25% of the lion's body weight. For a 200kg lion that means up to 50kg of meat! This is the same as a human eating 12-15 whole chickens in one go.

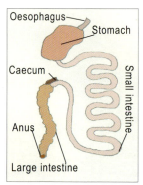

The digestive system of a carnivore is very simple compared to plant eaters.

The guts of carnivores in general are quite short, both the small intestine and the large intestine. The caecum, as in humans, is a mere vestige or completely absent. Some of the hair and bones pass through the gut but many carnivores regurgitate, especially the fur. The first defecation made by lions after a kill takes place within a few hours. It is a runny liquid and pitch black like tar, probably mostly made up of blood, and it smells!

Hyaenas vs Wild dogs Wild dogs and jackals regurgitate food for their pups. Amazingly, they can even regurgitate after a few hours, provided that they keep moving. Once they rest, digestion kicks in and they cannot regurgigate anymore. Hyaenas have the strongest digestive juices of all animals, being able to digest bone and even hoofs (not hair). Their digestive juices are so strong and start to work immediately, making it impossible for them to regurgitate their food. They have compensated by developing a long neck, very strong neck muscles and high forequarters to enable them to carry their food back to the den.

Ratio of volume:surface area

Imagine three 'cubic block animals' in the desert. If each cubic block is filled with water and left in the sun where they can lose water on all sides, which one will dry out first? Without giving it much thought, the answer should be - the smallest one. But there is a reason for this and that has to do with the ratio of volume:surface area. It is quite clear from the diagram that the surface area of a small animal is much larger (1:6) in relation to that of a large animal (1:2). In other words, there is much more surface area from which evaporation can take place in a small animal. It also has the problem that it will heat up quicker. The same applies to live animals.

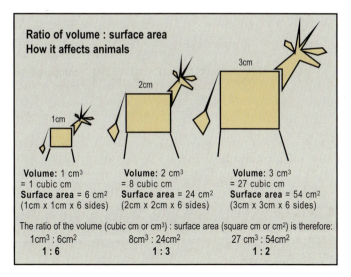

Ratio of volume : surface area
How it affects animals

Volume: 1 cm³
= 1 cubic cm
Surface area = 6 cm²
(1cm x 1cm x 6 sides)

Volume: 2 cm³
= 8 cubic cm
Surface area = 24 cm²
(2cm x 2cm x 6 sides)

Volume: 3 cm³
= 27 cubic cm
Surface area = 54 cm²
(3cm x 3cm x 6 sides)

The ratio of the volume (cubic cm or cm³) : surface area (square cm or cm²) is therefore:
1cm³ : 6cm²   8cm³ : 24cm²   27 cm³ : 54cm²
1 : 6   **1 : 3**   **1 : 2**

The disadvantage of a small body size

Now imagine real animals in the desert where there is no surface water available. Smaller animals are at an immediate disadvantage and one wonders how they manage to cope under heat stress. The answer lies in the metabolism of an animal, which is in direct correlation with the heart rate.

Heart rate and metabolism
Most herbivores are similar in that the heart size is proportionate to their body size. Their hearts comprise just above 0,5% of their body weight. The heart of a 4 ton elephant therefore weighs approximately 20kg and that of a 300kg zebra about 1,5kg. The function of the heart is to supply all body tissues with oxygen. If the body needs more oxygen, the volume of each heart beat cannot be altered because the heart is a constant (±0,5% of the body weight). It can, however, be achieved by adjusting the heart rate - in other words the number of beats per minute. That is why, during exercise, more oxygen is required and the heart rate thus increases. An increased heart rate results in an increase in metabolic rate. As was illustrated earlier, the smaller animal is at a disadvantage and thus needs more metabolic energy to cope - and thus has a faster heart rate or metabolic rate. Some of the smallest mammals, like some shrews, have a heart rate of up to 1 000 times per minute! However, to maintain a faster metabolism, they need to eat much more in relation to their body size than a large animal. A shrew will die of starvation if it is deprived of food even for a few hours. They have a very short lifespan of only 2-3 years.

The advantage of a large body size
A 4 ton elephant is a million times larger than a 4 gram shrew. A shrew eats about half its body weight (50%) in food per day, suggesting that a million shrews will eat two tons of food per day. Had it been a simple calculation of relativity one could say a four ton elephant will eat 2 tons (2 000kg) of food per day. However, an elephant eats only about 6-8% of its body weight in fresh food material, amounting to only 320kg - that is about one sixth of what a million shrews would eat! The reason why an elephant can cope on relatively less food, is because of its slow metabolic rate. This illustrates the advantage of having mega-herbivores (the plant-eating giants) as well as other large herbivores in an ecosystem. Because of their slower metabolism, their food requirements are far less per unit of body weight.

Ratio of body size : metabolic rate
The graph below gives a visual impression of how rapidly metabolic rate increases with decreasing body size (Schmidt-Nielsen, 1978).

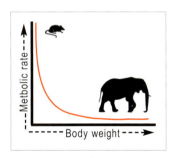

This graph shows how metabolic rate increases with a decrease in body weight.

WHAT IS THERMOREGULATION

Thermoregulation   Thermoregulation is the physiological and behavioural adaptations of animals to control their body heat. In very cold climates animals employ certain measures, even as drastic as hibernation. In Africa the biggest problem is coping with heat. The section below provides the most important adaptations of the semi-desert animals described in this book, such as the eland, gemsbok, red hartebeest, wildebeest and springbok. However, it is not only these animals that employ heat-controlling measures, most animals share at least some of the adaptations below, even some of the rodents. Rodents have overcome much of the problem by using cool, subterranean escapes. Animals that need to run very fast or very far to catch their prey, like wild dog and cheetah, also have a countercurrent heat exhange system (*rete mirabile*), to cool blood going to the brain. In fact, all carnivores and antelopes employ this mechanism after a sprint.

PHYSIOLOGICAL ADAPTATIONS TO CONSERVE WATER

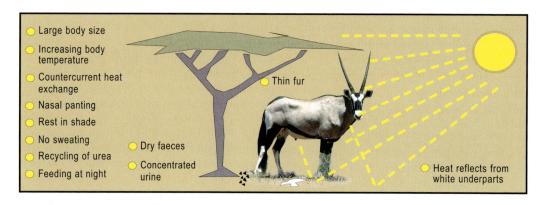

- Large body size
- Increasing body temperature
- Countercurrent heat exchange
- Nasal panting
- Rest in shade
- No sweating
- Recycling of urea
- Feeding at night
- Dry faeces
- Concentrated urine
- Thin fur
- Heat reflects from white underparts

Large body size   A large body has the advantage that it reaches its maximum body temperature only towards the end of the day. The excess heat is easily disposed of as soon as the ambient temperature becomes cooler. This is clearly illustrated by the gemsbok's behaviour at dusk when it seeks out higher ground to cool its body, often against a dune. A smaller body size has a disadvantage in that it heats up quicker (refer to pg 24).

Increasing body temperature   Some large antelope like the eland and the gemsbok have the ability to let their body temperature rise to as much as 43°C or in extreme cases to 46,5°C (Spinach,1986). In this way the body temperature is higher than that of the environment, and heat is actually lost instead of gained and no water is lost through sweating. Interestingly, the African wild dog also employs this method when chasing its prey for long distances.

Nasal panting   By closed-mouth panting, air is allowed to flow in and out across the nasal mucosa, which results in the evaporation of moisture in the nasal mucosa and the cooling of the venous blood close to the surface. The increase of body temperature and nasal panting are always employed together to prevent the increased blood temperature from damaging the brain, which would ultimately lead to the animal's death. Venous blood goes to the heart and arterial blood goes from the heart to the different organs, including the brain. The cool venous blood from the nasal mucosa thus cannot go directly to the brain but it can at least cool the arterial blood that goes to the brain. This is achieved by a system of countercurrent heat exchange (read below).

Countercurrent heat exchange   The countercurrent heat exchange system works on the same principle as a radiator. Blood is carried from the heart to the brain by the carotid artery. The temperature of the arterial blood is very high. Before entering the brain, the artery splits into a network of arterioles that are intertwined with a network of veins that flow in the opposite direction. The venal blood comes from the nasal passages, where it is cooled by evaporative cooling caused by nasal panting. This countercurrent network system is situated at the base of the brain. It is only about the size of a pea, but very effective, having the

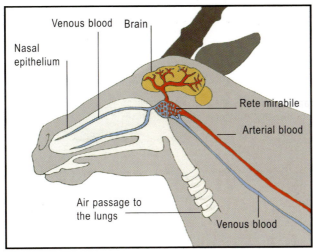

The countercurrent heat exchange mechanism situated at the base of the brain is called the 'rete mirabile'

ability to reduce the blood temperature by about 3°C. All carnivores and antelopes employ this mechanism, particularly after a sprint.

With this combined system, the panting animal is provided with a major advantage over an animal that cools itself by sweating. It has the advantage of being able to maintain a high body and skin temperature without adversely affecting the brain, thereby reducing the gradient between the skin temperature and the environment, so that less water is lost through evaporation. In extreme cases the animal can actually lose heat to the environment as the skin temperature may become higher than the ambient temperature (see 'Large body size').

Sweating The sweating animal loses large amounts of water through the skin, which has the function of cooling the body through evaporation. This kind of cooling system requires that the animal cools its entire body to the temperature it wishes to maintain in its brain, which in turn requires vast amounts of water. The lower skin temperature encourages heat flow from the environment to the body, which just warms the body up again. If water is abundant, this system is very effective and the sweating animal will cope well. The waterbuck is the best example of an animal that uses only sweating to lower its body temperature. Studies showed that under severe heat stress it will lose as much as 60 litre of water in one day! Compare this with a gemsbok that will only lose only ±4 litre under the same circumstances.

Thin fur Thin fur is beneficial when disposing of excess heat. Thus, semi-desert antelope like springbok, eland and gemsbok have very thin fur

as opposed to the antelopes associated with water such as the sitatunga, lechwe, reedbuck, waterbuck and puku (*Reduncinae*).

Reflecting heat A short, smooth and light-coloured coat helps to reflect heat instead of absorbing it. That is why the semi-desert antelopes like springbok, gemsbok and eland are light in colour. The white colouring underneath the stomach of the springbok and gemsbok is particularly effective in reflecting heat radiating from the ground. The thick, 'pronk' hairs on the springbok's rump, have the purpose of insulating the body.

Feeding at night By feeding at night an animal can increase its water intake. Condensation of air vapour can increase the water content of vegetation by as much as 40%.

Concentrating urine Desert animals have more effective kidneys than other mammals. The function of kidneys is to get rid of waste products. The kidneys of desert animals enable them to do this with the least loss of water. They produce only a few drops of very concentrated urine at a time, especially when heat-stressed.

Producing dry faeces Desert animals have the ability to produce very dry faeces in the form of small, single pellets.

Recycling urea and reabsorption of water Desert animals, in particular, which feed mainly on poor quality roughage, use urea cycling to provide their bodies with more protein. Normally, animals get rid of the poisonous ammonia (a by-product in the digestive tract), by converting it to urea and excreting it in urine together with water. In ruminants, not all the urea is excreted as some of it re-enters the rumen through the rumen wall or through the saliva. In the rumen it is again broken down into ammonia where the micro-organisms convert it to aminoacids. The latter are easily absorbed into the system as protein building blocks. Urea cycling is exceptionally well developed in the gemsbok. There is an additional benefit to this - if there is less urea to get rid of, less water will be required and at the same time, the maximum amount of energy will be obtained from their diet. That is why desert herbivores can survive on a diet much lower in protein than other herbivores.

NON-RUMINANTS

Order PROBOSCIDAE

Family ELEPHANTIDAE

African elephant

The only two members of this order are the African and Indian elephant. They have ever-growing incisor teeth, known as tusks, and a muscular appendage that is in fact an extension of the nose - the trunk. Elephants are hind-gut fermenters and they have a relatively fast turnover of food. This means they need to feed for longer than foregut fermenters, such as ruminants.

Order WHIPPOMORPHA

Suborder ANCODONTA

Family HIPPOPOTAMIDAE

Hippopotamus

Hippos were previously in the order *Artiodactyla* (even-toed animals) but have now been placed in a new order with whales and dolphins (*Whippomorpha*). The hippo is a foregut fermenter but unlike other foregut fermenters, the hippo does not ruminate. The *Artiodactyla* does not exist as an order anymore.

Order PERISSODACTYLA

Family EQUIDAE

Family RHINOCEROTIDAE

Zebra

White rhinoceros

Black rhinoceros

The order *Perissodactyla* comprises odd-toed animals. The rhinos have retained three toes, digits 2,3 and 4. The equids have only retained the middle digit (3) and only vestiges of digits 2 and 4 are evident as splint bones. The rhinos have lost their incisor and canine teeth and only have very large premolars and molars for grinding their food. The equids (horses and zebras) have retained both upper and lower incisors. This enables them to bite off course grass stems. Both the *Equidae* and *Rhinocerotidae* are hind-gut fermenters. Fermentation of tough plant material takes place in the caecum after the food has left the stomach.

Order SUIFORMES

Family SUIDAE

Subfamily Suinae

Subfamily Phacochoerinae

Warthog

Bushpig

The order *Suiformes* is generally known as the pig family. They have barrel-shaped bodies with short legs and large heads. The large head is used for rooting and fighting. The tubular snout is reinforced with a tough disk for rooting. All pigs have well-developed canines that in some, like the warthog, form tusks. The weight is carried on the two central toes (digits 3 and 4). Digits 2 and 5 are higher up the leg and splay out in soft mud to prevent them from sinking. They are hind-gut fermenters (fermentation takes place after the food has left the stomach).

African elephant

(Loxodonto africana)

Setswana: Tlou	**Afrikaans:** Olifant	**German:** Afrikanischer Elefant
French: L'Elaphant	**Spanish:** Elefante	**Italian:** Elefante

Photo Shellie Roodt

Did you know?

Musth gland The musth gland is situated between the ear opening and the eye. The word 'musth' is derived from a Hindi word that means 'intoxicated', in obvious reference to erratic behaviour. In Asian elephants the secretion is indeed associated with sexual aggression and is limited to males only. In African elephants, both male, female and even juveniles secrete an oily substance. There seems to be two kinds, one which is emitted by both sexes and related to stress and anxiety. The other is associated only with adult males and is related to sexual cycles. In both cases the gland is under autonomic control. This means it is an involuntary action (like the smooth muscles of the stomach) that is triggered by internal stimuli. There are strong suggestions that the 'stress secretion' is triggered by releases of adrenaline and the 'sexual secretion' by high testosterone levels (Estes, 1996). The latter kind is usually accompanied by a constant dribble from the penis and sometimes by aggressive behaviour. In African elephants, specifically, this phenomenon requires more research to be fully understood.

Heart The heart of an elephant weighs ±0,5% of its body weight. This is very similar in all mammals, except in humans, where it weighs ±0,4%. For a 4 000kg elephant the heart thus weighs ±20kg (Eltringham, 1993).

Compared to Blue whale Although the elephant is the largest land mammal, the Blue whale is the largest mammal. The heaviest recorded Blue whale weighed ±190 tons - this is as much as ±35 elephants!

Speed An elephant can run ±30-40km/hr. The fastest human runs only ±36km/hr.

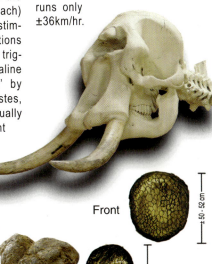

Front

Back

±50 - 52 cm

±52 - 58 cm

Order PROBOSCIDAE
Family ELEPHANTIDAE

Shoulder height m ±350-400cm, f ±300-330cm.
Weight m ±5 500-6 000kg, f ±3 600-4 000kg.
Gestation ±22 months.
Life span ±65 years.
Litter size One.
Habitat Woodland savanna, riverine woodland.
Food Grass, leaves, branches, bark and fruit.
Water requirements They need to drink regularly, ±100-300l/day.
Social structure Gregarious: Large, matriarchal breeding herds (±10-50), old-male herds (±5-8) and solitary males.
Sexual differences Males are larger with bigger tusks.
Active period Day and night.
Enemies Lion and man.
Voice Trumpeting and low rumbles made with the larynx.
Dentition I1/1 C0/0 P0/0 M6/6 = 28

Hippopotamus *(Hippopotamus amphibius)*

Setswana: Kubu	**Afrikaans:** Seekoei	**German:** Flusspferd
French: L'Hippopotame amphibie	**Spanish:** Hipopótamo	**Italian:** Ippopotamo

Did you know?

Sweat glands Hippos have no sweat or scent glands but they do have sub-dermal mucous glands secreting a viscous, red fluid - often referred to as 'blood sweat'. It dries like lacquer and serves to protect the thin epidermis against sunburn and water-loss, keeping it pliable and soft. The pinkish tinge is particularly noticeable in winter when they bask in the sun.

Lack of buoyancy and 'swimming' It is almost impossible for hippos to float,

therefore they need shallow water so that their back legs can touch the bottom when lying in it. They are not able to swim in the true sense, but they propel themselves using their hind legs and their tail as a rudder. They have 'paths' on the bottom where they 'walk-swim'.

Staying under water Hippos cannot breathe under water but an adult can stay submerged for ±5 minutes. This is only possible because they have the ability to let their pulse rate drop from ±60 to ±20 beats / minute (Carnaby, 2006). Their nostrils have muscles on the edges, enabling them to close. They also fold their ears back.

Metabolic rate and food requirements Because of their large size and low expenditure of energy, hippos have a very slow metabolism and need much less food per kg of body weight than any other herbivore. They can subsist on only 130kg of wet matter per night, and this often takes two days to digest.

Breeding Mating takes place in shallow water where much of the weight of the heavier male is absorbed by

the water. Infants are borne on dryland or in shallow water but are well adapted to suckle under water. A hand-reared calf instinctively takes a deep breath before starting to drink from a bottle, closes its nostrils and folds its ears flat as if it was suckling under water.

Order WHIPPOMORPHA
Suborder ANCODONTA
Family HIPPOPOTAMIDAE

Shoulder height m ±150cm, f ±144cm.
Weight m ±1 000-2 000kg, f ±900-1 700kg.
Gestation ±7-8 months.
Life span ±40 years.
Litter size One.
Habitat Open permanent water and sufficient short grass.
Food Grass - ±130kg / night.
Water requirements They are totally water dependent in terms of habitat. They also drink water.
Social structure Gregarious, pods of ±15-30 members with a female leader and territorial bull.
Sexual differences Males are larger than females.
Active period Nocturnal.
Enemies Lion.
Voice A deep repeated bellow.
Dentition I2/2 C1/1 P3-4/3-4 M3/3 = 36 - 40.

±24 cm

(*Equus burchelli*)

Zebra

Setswana: Pitse yanaga	**Afrikaans:** Bontkwagga	**German:** Steppenzebra
French: Le Zèbra de steppe	**Spanish:** Zebra	**Italian:** Zebra

Did you know?

Thermoregulation Studies have shown that there are subcutaneous fat accumulations primarily under the black stripes, which have the function of isolating heat (Bothma et. al, 1996). Other studies, referred to by Carnaby, 2006, have found that there is a greater concentration of capillaries below the black stripes. Black absorbs heat and white reflects it. The temperature above the white stripes is thus higher, causing a pressure gradient, which in turn causes the air to flow from the white stripes to the black stripes. This movement of air has a cooling effect on the capillaries close to the skin, and therefore a cooling effect on the animal. The subcutaneous fat layer presumably prevents the absorbed heat from penetrating any further than the skin surface. The lighter colour of the rump has the function of reflecting heat from the sun. When feeding during the heat of the day, zebras will almost always create their own shade by turning their back to the sun.

Ticks A normal, healthy zebra carries about 4 000 ticks of different species on its body without any ill effect to the animal. The impregnated female tick, fully gorged, falls to the ground where she lays her eggs in the ground. After hatching the minute ticks climb on grass stalks to await another host.

Digestive tract The zebra is a hind-gut fermenter with a single stomach and fermentation takes place in the caecum. The digestive organs of a ruminant represent ± 40% of its total body weight and in equids only ±15%. Digestion takes about 30-45 hours in equids and 70-100 hours in cattle.

Order PERISSODACTYLA
Family EQUIDAE

Shoulder height m/f ±135cm,
Weight m ±325kg, f ±300kg.
Gestation ±12½ months.
Life span ±35 years.
Litter size One.
Habitat Open savanna with sufficient grass and water.
Food Tall and short grass.
Water requirements They need to drink regularly, and require ±12 litres / day.
Social structure Gregarious: One-stallion harems, small stallion groups and solitary males.
Sexual differences Males are slightly heavier than females.
Active period Diurnal.
Enemies Lion, cheetah and spotted hyaena.
Voice A "qua-ha-ha" whinny .
Dentition I3/3 C0-1/0-1 P3/3 M3/3 = 36-40

±10.5 - 11.5 cm

White rhinoceros *(Ceratotherium simum)*

Setswana: Tshukudu	**Afrikaans:** Witrenoster	**German:** Breitmaulnashorn
French: Le Rhinosérus blanc	**Spanish:** Rinoceronte	**Italian:** Rinoceronte

Did you know?

Skeleton The rhino has a rigid spine and a short neck to enable it to maintain its balance when galloping. Their flexibility and strength are improved in that each vertebrae has a slot at the back into which the following spine fits lengthwise. When galloping, the head is held high and this requires tremendous muscle power. The power of the muscles is augmented by the hypertrophied nuchal ligament, which stretches from the high occipital crest to the elongated spines of the vertebrae. When the head is raised, a tight constriction is caused at the back of the neck where the hypertrophied nuchal ligament is attached, giving the white rhino the characteristic hump (the black rhino lacks this).

Droppings Both male and female make use of middens, but only the male kicks the dung or drags its feet to spread the scent around the territory. The dung can be found throughout the territory but the urine is spread only along the boundaries.

Genitalia Male and female rhinos have backward-facing genitalia and both sexes have the ability to squirt urine in powerful gushes. Males have undescended testes, lacking a scrotum.

Thermoregulation Rhinos are capable of sweating for evaporative cooling and the sweat is quite evident on the body surface on very hot days. Their physiology is not designed to conserve water. This is evident in the copious amounts of urine sprayed for scent marking.

Senses The rhino's sense of smell is well developed and its olfactory chamber is exceptionally large. The chamber is situated beneath the nasal bones, which are well buttressed to take the force of the horn when fighting. Their hearing is good, aided by movable ears that funnel the sound. They rely less on eye-sight than on other senses.

Order PERISSODACTYLA
Family RHINOCEROTIDAE

Shoulder height m ±200cm, f ±160cm.
Weight m ±2 000-2 300kg, f ±1 400-1 600kg.
Gestation ±16 months.
Life span ±45 years.
Litter size One.
Habitat Open savannah with patches of short grass, water and thickets for cover.
Food Short to medium grasses.
Water requirements They drink regularly, ±72 litres / day, but can go without for 2-3 days.
Social structure Males and females are territorial and have separate, overlapping territories.
Sexual differences Males are larger than females.
Active period Diurnal.
Enemies Man and lion.
Voice Growl, snort and puff.
Dentition I0/0 C0/0 P3/3 M3/3 = 24

±26 - 30 cm

(Diceros bicornis) **Black rhinoceros**

Setswana: Tshukudu	**Afrikaans:** Swartrenoster	**German:** Spitzmaulnashorn
French: Le Rhinceros Noir	**Spanish:** Rinoceronte	**Italian:** Rinoceronte

Did you know?

Horns The horns of rhinos are composed of a mass of tubular filaments that can be compared in substance to hair. The horn is not attached to the bone, but like hair, it grows from the skin. The skull is rough below the horn to allow firm attachment. The horns are ever-growing and grow at ±6-10cm per year. There are no nerves present, which makes it possible to saw off the horn without pain to the animal. This is done in some wildlife areas as an extreme measure to prevent poaching. Some poachers in South Africa (with a conscience, I suppose) recently darted rhino to obtain the horn without killing them. The horns reach astronomical prices on the black market for use as an aphrodisiac (Far East) and for dagger handles (Yemen).

Parasites When rolling in mud or ash for protection, rhinos often miss the skin behind the shoulders - the most common place for rhino sores. These are very prevalent on black rhinos and are mostly caused by the filaria parasite. This is a nematode parasite that has a fly as an intermediate host. The lesions become blood-encrusted and ulcerated and are often aggravated by oxpecker (a bird) activity.

Resting They may lie flat on their sides when resting - a position never used by white rhinos.

Rolling over
Rhinos cannot roll over because of the prominent spine.

They have to first stand up and then lie down on the other side.

Calf At first a calf suckles standing up but as it gets bigger, it has to lie down to reach. It suckles for about one year. The calf usually keeps behind or to the side of the mother, unlike the White rhino, where the calf walks infront.

Social structure They are mainly solitary, the only association being between mother and calf, which can last from two to four years. They are strictly territorial but may have overlapping home ranges.

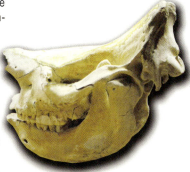

±22-24 cm

Order PERISSODACTYLA
Family RHINOCEROTIDAE

Shoulder height m/f ±1,6m high.
Weight m ±750-950kg, f ± 780-1 000kg.
Gestation ±15-16 months.
Life span ± 40 years.
Litter size One.
Habitat Areas with dense shrubs and plenty of water.
Food Leaves, fruit and twigs.
Water requirements They need to drink ±35 litres per day, but can survive with 2-3 day intervals.
Social structure Usually solitary or a cow with her calf.
Sexual differences Males are slightly smaller than females.
Active period Dawn and dusk, drink in the evening.
Enemies Lion.
Voice Snort, growl and scream.
Dentition I0/0 C0/0 P3/3 M3/3 = 24

Warthog (*Phacochoerus africanus*)

Setswana: Kolobe	**Afrikaans:** Vlakvark	**German:** Warzenschwein
French: Le Phacochère	**Spanish:** Farocero	**Italian:** Facocero

Did you know?

Anatomy The warthog's head is large compared to the body and therefore the bone surface behind the braincase (supra occipital crest), is elongated to support the attachment of the massive neck muscles. These muscles provide the power necessary for the upward motion when digging for roots and when fighting. The 'warts' on the face are to buttress the fighting blows and to protect against predators. Males have two pairs of warts and females only one. The tusks are elongated canine teeth and are used for fighting and rooting. By kneeling down, a firm base for the leverage of the head is provided. The skin on the front leg joints is hardened to form protective calluses. These calluses are even evident in embryos. The snout is elongated, consisting of a hardened cartilaginous disc, with nostrils that can close to prevent soil from entering whilst the warthog is rooting.

Unique feeding strata Of all the herbivores, only the warthog and the hippo go without feeding for at least 12 hours of the day. The hippo is inactive with a slow metabolism, but how does the warthog manage? This animal has successfully eliminated much of its competition by using an underground plant resource - roots and rhizomes. The only competition is earthworms, insects, moles and molerats. Rhizomes store valuable nutrients for the following growing season. By digging up this treasure chest, supplemented by earthworms and other sources of protein that are ingested accidentally, the warthog satisfies all its nutritive requirements and manages to fit in a midday rest, a wallow in a mud-pool and a good night's sleep in the safety of a den.

±3.5 - 4.5 cm

Order SUIFORMES
Family SUIDAE
Subfamily SUINAE

Shoulder height m ±70cm, f ±60cm.
Weight m ±60-100kg, f ±45-70kg.
Gestation ± 5¹/₂ months.
Life span ±20 years.
Litter size One to five.
Habitat Open areas around pans and savanna woodland.
Food Grass, wild fruit, succulent roots, insects, earthworms.
Water requirements They drink often, requiring ±3,5 litres / day.
Social structure Family groups, bachelor groups, solitary males.
Sexual differences Males are larger and have two pairs of warts on the face.
Active period Diurnal.
Enemies Lion, leopard, cheetah and wild dog.
Voice Growl, snort and grunt.
Dentition I1/2-3 C1/1 P3/2 M3/3 = 32-34.= 32-34.

(Potamochoerus porcus) # Bushpig

Setswana: Kolobe ye naga	**Afrikaans:** Bosvark	**German:** Buschschwei
French: Le Potamochere d'Afrique	**Spanish:** Jabali	**Italian:** Cinghiale

Did you know?

Food Like warthogs, bushpigs eat mainly roots of grasses, sedges, herbs, fruit, grubs and insects. However, while warthogs may occasionally nibble at a carcass, bushpigs eat more meat, even killing birds and rodents. They have the ability to smell a carcass from a long distance. There is a record of a leopard being chased off its kill by a bushpig and they will attack injured animals with open wounds. They roll away large logs to get to the grubs underneath and have been observed combining forces to do this. This requires enormous strength, therefore the neck muscles are extremely powerful. Similar to the white rhino, the spines on the shoulder are elongated to offer attachment for these strong muscles, forming the characteristic hump.

Swimming Bushpigs are very good swimmers. This was recorded by Child during the flooding of Lake Kariba in Zimbabwe, where they were seen swimming strongly more than 1km from the dryland. Since their nose is carried way below the shoulders in the walking position, they swim with their nose under the water and only come up for air every ±15 seconds.

Nests The female carries grass, twigs and shrubs to form a large haystack which she first compacts and then hollows out to provide both a soft base and sufficient insulation against the cold. These nests are large, ±1m high and 3m wide and may be in a crevice, among tree roots or under bushes.

Raising the young After birth the mother suckles the young but, shortly afterwards, the dominant boar takes over much of the responsibilities of raising and taking care of them. When they are old enough to forage, he is the one who accompanies them and he will aggressively defend them against predators.

Order SUIFORMES
Family SUIDAE
Subfamily SUINAE

Shoulder height m/ f ±75cm.
Weight m ±82kg, f ±48-66kg.
Gestation ±4 months.
Life span ±15 years.
Litter size Three to six.
Habitat Thickets, forests, riverine under-bush and reedbeds, always close to water.
Food Bulbs, tubers, rhizomes, fruit, carrion and fresh meat.
Water requirements They usually get enough from food, but will also drink.
Social structure Small groups of 6-12 with males, females and young animals.
Sexual differences Males are larger than females.
Active period Strictly nocturnal.
Enemies Leopard, lion, wild dog and hyaena.
Voice A long resonant growl as alarm call, snort, sniff.
Dentition I3/3 C1/1 P4-3/3-4 M3/3 = 40, 42, 44.

R U M I N A N T S

Order RUMINANTEA

Family GIRAFFIDAE

Giraffe

Family BOVIDAE

Subfamily Antilopinae

Tribe Alcelaphini

Wildebeest   Tsessebe   Red Hartebeest

Tribe Hippotragini

Oryx   Roan antelope   Sable antelope

Tribe Reduncini

Lechwe   Puku   Waterbuck   Common reedbuck   Mountain reeduck

Tribe Aepycerotini

Impala

Tribe Antilopini

Oribi   Springbuck   Steenbok

Tribe Cephalophini

Duiker

Tribe Oreotragini

Klipspringer

Subfamily Bovinae

Tribe Bovini

Buffalo

Tribe Tragelaphini

Eland

Kudu

Nyala

Sitatunga

Bushbuck

The order *Ruminantea* was previously part of the order *Artiodactyla* (even-toed animals), which included pigs and the hippo. All the ruminants have now been placed in the order - *Ruminantea*. The order *Artiodactyla* does not exist anymore. The ruminants are foregut fermenters that remasticate their food (chew the cud). This order includes both grazers (grass-eating animals) and browsers (leaf-eating animals). Their dentition and skulls are also very similar. They do not have upper incisors but the lower incisors bite against a horny pad to reduce wear. They also have a large toothless gap between the incisors and the cheekteeth, called the 'diastema'. This is to accommodate a long tongue, which is essential for gathering food into the mouth.

Giraffe

(*Giraffa camelopardalis*)

Setswana: Thutlwa	**Afrikaans:** Kameelperd	**German:** Giraffe
French: La Girafe	**Spanish:** Jirafa	**Italian:** Giraffa

Did you know?

Bloodflow The unusual shape of the giraffe requires extreme adaptations to regulate the bloodflow. Firstly the systolic blood pressure, which is the pressure at the level of the heart, needs to be very high to reach the head. During tests, pressures of 260mm Hg (35kPa) were measured. Compare this with 100mm Hg (13kPa) in humans. To withstand that pressure, the arterial system has very thick walls and the venous system is equipped throughout with valves that help with the return of blood from the limbs. Those valves also prevent backflow to the brain when the head is lowered.

Order RUMINANTIA
Family GIRAFFIDAE

Shoulder height m ±300cm, f ±280cm.
Weight m ±1200kg, f ±800kg.
Gestation ±15 months.
Life span ±28 years.
Litter size One.
Habitat Mostly *Acacia* savanna woodland with permanent water.
Food Leaves, fruit, flowers and twigs of trees and shrubs.
Water requirements They need to drink regularly, ±40 litres / day.
Social structure Gregarious. Small herds of 3-10 with a loose structure, also solitary males.
Sexual differences Males are heavier than females.
Active period Diurnal.
Enemies Lion, cheetah, leopard and hyaena.
Voice An alarm snort or grunt.
Dentition I0/3 C0/1 P3/3 M3/3 = 32

Horns The paired horns of giraffes are quite unlike antelope horns in that they are present at birth and even during the embryo stage. They are formed from car-tilage of dermal (skin) origin and are not at first attached to the skull. At birth they are soft and lie against the skull but after a few days they stand erect and a process of bone deposition starts to take place. Growth takes place at the base of the horn but bone deposition starts from the tips downward. Fusion with the skull only takes place after ±4-4,5 years in males and after ±7 years in females. Old males devel-op additional outgrowths on the fore-head and behind the ears.

Locomotion When walking, the two legs on the same side move together so that the entire weight of the giraffe is supported first on the one side, then on the other, similar to a camel. Their long legs and short body would cause them to trip if they had a normal gait - left front, right back, right front, left back.

Voice They are not voiceless as is popularly believed, but they occasionally grunt, snort, bleat and emit flute-like notes.

Muzzle and tongue
The tongue is about 45cm long. Both the tongue and the lips are covered by horny papillae to protect them against the vicious thorns of the *Acacia* trees.

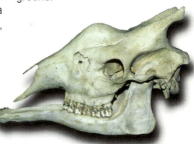

Giving birth A giraffe gives birth standing up, which means the baby has to fall ±2m to the ground!

±19 cm

African buffalo
(Syncerus caffer)

Setswana: Nare	**Afrikaans:** Buffel	**German:** Afrikanischer Büffel
French: Le Buffle d'Afrique	**Spanish:** Búfalo	**Italian:** Bufalo

Did you know?

Home range Buffaloes move loosely within well-defined home ranges, rather than territories. The size of the home range is not determined by social behaviour but rather by ecological restrictions (in other words availability of food and water).

Social structure They are gregarious and may form very large herds consisting of a number of stable sub-herds. The sub-herds consist of a few related cows with their off-spring as well as a varying number of adult and sub-adult bulls. The sex ratio within a large herd is usually maintained at about one:one. Generally, there are no strongly developed relationships between herd members, except between mother and offspring. The exchange of different herd members and splitting up and regrouping is common.

Sexual aggression There is a dominance hierarchy among males, but this relates to reproductive priority within the herd or the sub-herd, rather than defending the territory. There is almost no sexual rivalry within a herd - a safe survival strategy for animals that have the potential to kill each other in a dispute. Dominance is determined by size, similar to the Spiral-horned antelope. Non-breeding males are not actively driven out of the herd but leave spontaneously to join small groups. Even old, non-breeding bulls are not forcefully expelled from the herd, but they sometimes prefer to form separate groups, informally referred to as 'Daga-boys'.

Order RUMINANTIA
Family BOVIDAE
Subfamily BOVINAE
Tribe BOVINI

Shoulder height m ±160cm, f ±150cm.
Weight m ±750-820kg, f ±680-740kg.
Gestation ±11 months.
Life span ±23 years.
Litter size One.
Habitat Savannah with sufficient tall grasses, near water.
Food Tall grass - bulk roughage feeder.
Water requirements They are totally water dependent, requiring about 21,3 litres / day.
Social structure Gregarious, forming large, mixed herds, also solitary males and male herds.
Sexual differences Males are more heavily built and have heavier horns than females.
Active period At night and cooler parts of the day.
Enemies Lion.
Voice Bellow like cattle.
Dentition I0/3 C0/1 P3/3 M3/3 = 32

± 15-21 cm

What is 'Resource partitioning'?

WATER-LOVING ANTELOPE Resource partitioning is the ability of wild herbivores to share their resource. Each species is adapted to fill a specific niche (ecological position), where competition is limited and where they can enjoy the maximum benefit from their resource. The example below shows the water-loving antelope where reedbuck feed on tall, rough grasses, sitatunga feed on papyrus and other water plants. Lechwe move with the receding water, making use of the green grasses that appear as the water level drops. Puku and lechwe share almost the same habitat but puku prefers slightly higher ground. The waterbuck is absolutely dependent on the shade that marginal woodland offers and they feed on taller grasses.

Reedbuck - tall grassland near rivers.   *Sitatunga - papyrus and deep-water swamps.*   *Lechwe - aquatc meadow grass-land.*   *Puku - slightly raised ground near rivers.*   *Waterbuck - marginal woodland and taller grasses.*

BROWSERS Browser share their resource mainly by feeding at different levels. They also occupy different habitats, for example the giraffe prefers savanna woodland, the bushbuck and duiker prefer dense, riverine woodland, the klipspringer prefers koppies and the rhino prefers shrubland. The kudu is quite versatile and occupy most of the above.

Klipspringer - concentrate selector on rocky outcrops.   *Kudu - medium level browser in different habitats.*   *Giraffe - tall level browser in savanna woodland.*   *Black rhino - medium level browser of roughage in shrub-land.*   *Bushbuck - medium to low level concentrate selector in dense woodland.*   *Duiker - low level concentrate selector - dense woodland.*

FACILITATION Facilitation is where one animal opens up an area or 'mows' down the grass to make it more accessible to other species. Both buffalo and zebra eat tall grass, but buffalo strip the leaves off and zebras nip of the stem. The shorter stem will open up leaves closer to the ground, ideal for wildebeest. The impala, with its split upper lip can feed virtually at ground level.

Buffalo - bulk, roughage feeder that prefers tall grasses and eat mainly the leaves.   *Zebra - they can feed on tall and short grass. Upper and lower incisors enable them to bite off tough grass stems.*   *Wildebeest - short grass feeder, non-selective (broad muzzle).*   *Impala - the impala is very versatile. It has a split upper lip that makes it possible to feed at ground level.*

Greater kudu   (*Tragelaphus strepsiceros*)

Setswana: Tholo	**Afrikaans:** Koedoe	**German:** Grosskudu
French: Le Grand Kudu	**Spanish:** Kudu	**Italian:** Kudu

Did you know?

How tannins affect kudus

Increased tannin levels is a survival strategy employed by plants to deter browsers. Scientific studies have shown that the level of concentrated tannins in the leaves of the Sweet thorn (*Acacia caffra*)

increases by ±94% within 15 minutes while a browser is feeding on it. It was found that aromatic compounds are released when browsing pressure is applied. Other plant parts and even other plants in the vicinity react to this by increasing their own tannin levels. Kudus have adapted quite well to this by feeding on one plant for only a short period before moving on to the next. Browsers have also adapted to neutralise the tannins to a degree by increasing the levels of proline (an amino-acid) and non-hydrolysable fixed substances in their saliva (Bothma et.al, 1996). Herbivores in general have also adapted by developing larger livers to cope with the toxic elements in plants.

Importance of size The Tragelaphines, which include all the spiral-horned antelope, are non-territorial. Reproductive success takes priority over defending a resource or territory. Reproductive dominance is based on body size and the size of their horns. With the exception of the Bushbuck, male reproductive success is based on absolute domi-

nance over other males and not over a territory. In this group the horns continue to grow even after the animal reaches maturity, whereas in territorial species such as tsessebe and wildebeest, the horns reach their maximum size at maturity.

Order RUMINANTIA
Family BOVIDAE
Subfamily BOVINAE
Tribe TRAGELAPHINI

Shoulder height m ±150cm, f ±135cm.
Weight m ±190-270kg, f ±120-210kg.
Gestation ±7 months.
Life span ±14 years.
Litter size One.
Habitat Savanna woodland with enough trees, scrub and water.
Food Leaves, shoots, fruits and seed pods.
Water requirements They drink regularly, requiring ±9 litres / day.
Social structure Small herds of 5-12 animals of female and young. Males form separate herds, only joining to mate.
Sexual differences Only males have horns and are much larger.
Active period Diurnal.
Enemies Lion, leopard, wild dog and hyaena.
Voice A loud bark.
Dentition I0/3 C0/1 P3/3 M3/3 = 32

(Taurotragus oryx)

Eland

Setswana: Phofhu	Afrikaans: Eland	German: Elenantilope
French: L'Elan du Cap	Spanish: Elan	Italian: Antilope gigante

Did you know?

Thermoregulation The eland is adapted to inhabit very dry and hot areas. Because of its large size, its body does not heat up fast. During the night the body cools down. During the day it gradually warms up until about midday, when it actively has to start regulating its body temperature. It therefore only has to employ evaporative cooling for about five hours of the day - an effective adaptation to reduce water loss. During the absence of water, the eland has the amazing ability to allow its body temperature to rise by ±7°C. For a 500kg eland this equates to saving ±5l of water (Taylor, 1969). The water loss is further reduced by excreting dry faeces, by limiting the amount of water in the urine, by seeking shade during the hottest hours of the day and by lowering its metabolic rate. Eland need to be at rest and ruminate for ±50% of the day to achieve this successfully.

Clicking A large eland bull generates a most unusual clicking sound when walking. Estes (1984) suggests that it could be a tendon slipping over the knee or it can be the springing ligament in the fetlock joint (see pg 8). A San guide told me that it is caused by the two halves of the hoof that click together. He said the heavy shoulder weight of the male causes the hoof to splay and as it lifts its foot, the two halves jump back into place, makng the characteristic clicking sound. It occurs mostly in males, but it also occurs in large females. This phenomenon needs more research, but whatever causes it, the social significance is a vocal message that a large male is approaching. Where a number of males are attracted to a female in estrous, this is usually the cue for the younger males to make way.

Order RUMINANTIA
Family BOVIDAE
Subfamily BOVINAE
Tribe TRAGELAPHINI

Shoulder height m ±140-180cm, f ±130-150cm.
Weight m ±700kg, f ±470kg.
Gestation ±9 months.
Life span ±25 years in captivity.
Litter size One.
Habitat Very adaptable, from open bushveld to grassland, even mountainous areas.
Food Grass and leaves. Their narrow muzzle and digestive tract is adapted for food high in protein.
Water requirements They need ±23 litres / day but can go without if they eat tubers, bulbs and melons.
Social structure Gregarious with loose associations, herds varying from 10-200 animals.
Sexual differences Males are much larger but both have horns.
Active period Diurnal, but will feed at night.
Enemies Mainly lion.
Voice Alarm sneeze or a roaring snort.
Dentition I0/3 C0/1 P3/3 M3/3 = 32

±12.5 14 cm

Sitatunga

(*Tragelaphus speckei*)

Setswana: Naakong **Afrikaans:** Waterkoedoe **German:** Wasserkudu
French: Le Sitatunga **Spanish:** Sitatunga **Italian:** Palanca nera da papiro

Did you know?

Habitat The sitatunga is the only antelope adapted to survive in an entirely aquatic habitat. They occur in swamps and show a preference for papyrus communities.

Scent glands Most antelopes possess scent glands either on their heads, between their hooves or on the fetlock joint. The sitatunga and the waterbuck, both of which often stand in the water, have diffuse glands spread over most of the body to make the skin impermeable to water.

Hoofs The front hoofs are about 18cm long in an adult male and markedly splayed to provide an enlarged surface to traverse the aquatic vegetation and soft mud. The false hoofs, which can be seen above the true hoofs as horny protrusions, are greatly enlarged and the area between them and the true hoofs is covered by a swollen leathery pad. This facilitates a proper grip on the slippery mud if they need to make a quick get-away.

Social structure Sitatungas are gregarious and non-territorial. The females form herds of about six to seven, of which about three are adult females and the rest offspring. They may or may not be accompanied by an adult male. Adult males tend to avoid each other and they space themselves by loud barking. Yet, they do not defend a territory.

While feeding they are usually solitary but when threatened they seek safety in numbers. When hunted or wounded, they will completely submerge themselves in water with only the nostrils and eyes sticking out. During the day they often rest within the safety of the floating papyrus, where they open up platforms for themselves.

Food When the water is low, they eat papyrus umbles (flowerheads), almost exclusively. They also eat waterlilies, sedges, water grasses and leaves.

Order RUMINANTIA
Family BOVIDAE
Subfamily BOVINAE
Tribe TRAGELAPHINI

Shoulder height m ±110cm, f ±80cm.
Weight m ±114kg, f ±55kg.
Gestation ±7$^1/_2$ months.
Life span ±20 years in captivity.
Litter size One.
Habitat Permanently flooded areas with reeds or papyrus.
Food Papyrus umbels and aquatic grasses.
Water requirements They are totally dependent on water.
Social structure Usually solitary or pairs. Always connected to a loosely knit herd.
Sexual differences Only males have horns and are much larger.
Active period Day and night.
Enemies Crocodile, lion, python and leopard.
Voice Loud alarm bark, similar to bushbuck.
Dentition I0/3 C0/1 P3/3 M3/3 = 32

±8.5cm

(Tragelaphus scriptus) **Bushbuck**

Setswana: Ngurungu	**Afrikaans:** Bosbok	**German:** Schirrantilope
French: Le Guib/Antelope harnaché	**Spanish:** Antilope Jeroglifico	**Italian:**

Did you know?

Social structure Bushbuck differ from other *Tragelaphines* in that they are strictly solitary, the only associations being a female and her offspring. The reason for their solitary lifestyle is because of their specific habitat requirements which limit them to a strip of riverine bush. If they want to hold on to it, they have to remain there. They do not strictly defend a territory. They have a small, core area where they rest in safety but home ranges of different individuals do overlap. They often use the same lying-down place day after day. When they encounter a neighbour, it is usually friendly except during mating when males have been known to fight until death. However, fighting is rare. Like other *Tragelaphines*, bushbuck behaviour is aimed mainly at reproductive success and not at defending a territory (Estes, 1990).

Habitat They require thickly vegetated, undisturbed, riverine woodland. Areas which are over-utilised by elephants, livestock or other game, will cause bushbuck numbers to diminish. Like the oribi, steenbok and klipspringer, they ignore areas that are seasonally invaded by migratory species such as wildebeest and zebra. They actively seek out the safety of lodges and they are one of the few antelope to do this, becoming so tame that they even beg for food. Nowhere is this better illustrated than in Letaba camp in the Kruger Park.

Chobe bushbuck The Chobe bushbuck, which occurs in Botswana, is more reddish-brown in colour and they have more distinct spots and stripes. This is an area variation but they belong to the same species.

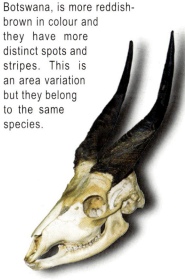

Order RUMINANTIA
Family BOVIDAE
Subfamily BOVINAE
Tribe TRAGELAPHINI

Shoulder height m ±80cm, f ±70cm.
Weight m ±40-77kg, f ±30-36kg.
Gestation ±6-7 months.
Life span ±11 years.
Litter size One.
Habitat Riverine bush and thickets near water.
Food Leaves and fruit, sometimes grass.
Water requirements Very dependent, requiring ±1,5 litres / day.
Social structure Solitary or pairs or small groups of females and their young.
Sexual differences Only males have horns and they are larger.
Active period Nocturnal, active at dawn and dusk, also diurnal.
Enemies Leopard, lion, wild dog, python, crocodile.
Voice A loud bark, like a baboon.
Dentition I0/3 C0/1 P3/3 M3/3 = 32

± 4-4.5 cm

Blue Wildebeest *(Connochaetus taurinus)*

Setswana: Kgokong	**Afrikaans:** Blouwildebees	**German:** Streifengnu
French: Le Gnou Bleu	**Spanish:** Ñu	**Italian:** Gnu

Did you know?

Territoriality Blue wildebeests have some of the smallest territories of all bovids because they naturally occur in huge aggregations where space is always a problem. They have evolved in such a way that a small space is sufficient for their needs. As a migratory animal their need is to secure a place to mate and not to defend their food resource.

Breeding bulls hold their territories all year round, although mating is restricted to the ±3 week rut. Only a third to a half of adult males hold territories.

Thermoregulation It is quite well documented that the gemsbok and the eland limit their water-loss during heat stress by allowing their body temperature to rise and by employing a countercurrent heat exchange system to cool the blood going to the brain. In fact, all large antelopes that occur in semi-desert areas employ this mechanism, the wildebeest being one of them. Most large antelope as well as sheep and cattle both sweat and pant, but a wildebeest only pants. This is a much more effective way of evaporative cooling because it minimises water loss (Louw, 1993).

Disease Bovine malignant catarrhal fever or 'snotsiekte' is a viral disease that affects cattle and can only be transmitted by wildebeest and sheep. It is now generally accepted that the wildebeest's role in spreading the disease was overrated in the past and that severe restrictions diminished their value unnecessarily. Their value on a game farm far outweighs the few individual animals they may affect.

Order RUMINANTIA
Family BOVIDAE
Subfamily ANTILOPINAE
Tribe ALCELAPHINI

Height m ±150cm, f ±135cm.
Weight m ±230-270kg, f ±170-200kg.
Gestation ±8 months.
Life span ±20 years.
Litter size One.
Habitat Open savanna with short grass and enough water.
Food Short grass up to 15cm.
Water requirements They need to drink regularly - ±9 litres /day.
Social structure Gregarious, mixed herds and bachelor herds. Territorial mainly when breeding.
Sexual differences Males are slightly larger than females.
Active period Diurnal, but will also feed at night.
Enemies Lion, leopard, cheetah and wild dog.
Voice A snort and a nasal 'gnu', earning them the name 'Gnu'.
Dentition I0/3 C0/1 P3/3 M3/3 = 32

(Damaliscus lunatus)

Tsessebe

Setswana: Tsessebe / Kabule	**Afrikaans:** Basterhartbees	**German:** Halbmondantilope
French: Le Tsessebe	**Spanish:** Damalisco	**Italian:** Damalisco

Did you know?

Social organisation The Tsessebe is gregarious, forming small herds of 4-10 mature animals and their offspring. They are territorial, maintaining territories by regular patrol. The territories are about 3km². They mark their territories by falling to their knees and rubbing their preorbital glands in the soil. They also mark grasses with this gland. The nursery herd remains permanently associated with the territorial male, unlike wildebeests. Male offspring are evicted by the territorial male at about one year of age, when they join established bachelor groups that remain on the periphery of the established territory (Joubert, 1972).

Order RUMINANTIA
Family BOVIDAE
Subfamily ANTILOPINAE
Tribe ALCELAPHINI

Height m/f ±125cm.
Weight m ±140kg, f ±126kg.
Gestation ±8 months.
Life span ±15 years.
Litter size One.
Habitat Ecotone between open grassy plains and woodland.
Food Medium short grasses.
Water requirements They need to drink regularly - ±5 litres /day.
Social structure Gregarious, small breeding herds, bachelor herds and territorial males.
Sexual differences Males are larger than females.
Active period Mostly diurnal.
Enemies Lion, cheetah, wild dog and hyaena.
Voice Snort.
Dentition I0/3 C0/1 P3/3 M3/3 = 32

Shoulder height The high forequarters of the tsessebe prevent it from feeding at ground level with ease. They usually feed at a higher level than the impala (±3cm). The group of antelopes known as the *Alcelaphines* have compensated for their high shoulders by developing an elongated skull.

Habitat They need grass, water and shade. They favour abrupt ecotones between grassland and woodland - an ecotone being an area where two vegetation types meet. Bush encroachment (usually the result of overgrazing) reduces their range and numbers.

Speed They take to the open when danger threatens, preferring to keep the predator in sight as they usually are able to outrun it. They have the reputation of being the fastest antelope and although they are indeed very fast, it has been found that they are probably no faster than any other plains antelope.

± 8 cm

Red hartebeest (*Alcelaphus buselaphus*)

Setswana: Kgama **Afrikaans:** Rooi hartebees **German:** Kuhantilope
French: Le Bubale tora **Spanish:** Alcelafo caama **Italian:** Congone

Did you know?

Body size They are fairly large in size - an advantage in the arid areas that they inhabit, as the body does not heat up so fast.

Muzzle The muzzle is narrow to enable them to feed more selectively.

Senses Their senses of smell and hearing are acute but

±8.5cm

their sight is not very good.

Habitat The red hartebeest is a typical plains antelope, occurring on various types of grassland. It will enter woodland more readily than the wildebeest but will stick to the boundaries. They prefer semi-desert associations such as the Kalahari with its dry grassland and scattered, low bushes.

Water requirements They can survive without surface water. During droughts they dig up succulent roots and bulbs and eat melons to meet their water requirements.

Social structure Males are territorial and they remain separate from the females except when actively herding. They defend their territories against other males.

Breeding They breed continuously, calving every 9-10 months with an eight-month pregnancy. The previous calf will stay with the mother, resulting in commonly seen mixed herds.

Thermoregulation The Red hartebeest employ a countercurrent heat exchange mechanism to cool blood going to the brain, like the gemsbok (see pg 26).

Order RUMINANTIA
Family BOVIDAE
Subfamily ANTILOPINAE
Tribe ALCELAPHINI

Shoulder height m ±120-130cm, f ± 105-115cm.
Weight m ±140 -180kg, f ±100-135kg.
Gestation ±8 months.
Life span ±14 years.
Litter size One.
Habitat Open areas in dry savannah and semi-arid areas.
Food Grass, preferring medium grasses.
Water requirements Survives with minimum water.
Social organization Gregarious, breeding herds with a male, male herds and solitary males.
Sexual differences Males are larger and have heavier horns.
Active period Early mornings and evenings.
Enemies Lion, leopard, wild dog and hyaena.
Voice A sneezing snort.
Dentition I0/3 C0/1 P3/3 M3/3 = 32

(Oryx gazelle)

Gemsbok / Oryx

Setswana: Kukama	**Afrikaans:** Gemsbok	**German:** Oryxantilope
French: L'Oryx	**Spanish:** Oryx	**Italian:** Oryx

Did you know?

Dentition The broad, high-crowned molars are specifically adapted to withstand wear caused by the tough desert

> **Order** RUMINANTIA
> **Family** BOVIDAE
> **Subfamily** ANTILOPINAE
> **Tribe** HIPPOTRAGINI

Shoulder height m ±120cm; f ±110 cm.
Weight m ±240kg, f ±210kg.
Gestation ± 9 months.
Life span ± 19 years.
Litter size One.
Habitat Open plains in semi-dessert and dry savanna.
Food Grass, succulent tubers and tsamma melons.
Water requirements They can survive on very little surface water have certain adapations (see pg 24).
Social organization Gregarious, territorial males, small male herds and mixed herds.
Sexual differences Males are heavier but females often have longer but thinner horns.
Active period Diurnal and nocturnal
Enemies Lion, wild dog and spotted hyaena
Voice Bellow like cattle
Dentition I0/3 C0/1 P3/3 M3/3 = 32

grasses. The wide row of incisor teeth allows them to crop the coarse grasses, which in semi-desert regions grow very close to the ground.

Muzzle The oryx has the smallest muzzle of all large-bodied, true grazers, allowing them to select the nutritious and tasty parts of the plants.

Social structure The gemsbok is gregarious, forming small or large herds. Some males are solitary and territorial but the majority occur in mixed herds. In the mixed herds the males establish a dominance hierarchy but the territorial male is still the most dominant. The territorial males are quite tolerant of non-territorial males

Food retension The gemsbok retains its food for longer to extract the maximum amount of protein. The longer the food stays in the rumen, the more effective the fermentation process and the more protein will be made available to the animal. A gemsbok retains its food in the rumen for a record time of just

over three days (about 75 hours) before it is passed on to the rest of the digestive tract. The extended food retention, however, creates a problem in that the animal cannot compensate for the low protein value by eating more food, since the rumen can only hold a certain quantity of food at a time. Under severe conditions, an animal will thus die - not because of a shortage of food, but because of the inability to process the food fast enough to obtain the required amount of protein.

Thermoregulation (See pg 25).

±10.3-11.5 cm

Roan antelope   *(Hippotragus equinus)*

Setswana: Kwalala etsetsa	**Afrikaans:** Bastergemsbok	**German:** Pferdeantilope
French: Antilope rouanne	**Spanish:** Antilope Ruano	**Italian:** Antilope roana

Did you know?

Shoulder height With their slightly raised shoulders, they are better adapted to feed on medium to tall grasses.

Habitat Roan antelope are rare compared to other antelope and there are three main reasons for it: *Highly specific:* They are highly specific in their habitat requirements and any changes caused by overgrazing, trampling, fire etc., will cause them to seek new feeding grounds. *Large home range:* Their home ranges are large - up to 100km^2 - and there is seldom an overlap, explaining why their distribution is often patchy and discontinuous. *Low biomass:* They have evolved to use areas that cannot support a high biomass - in this case tall grassland.

Social structure

They form small herds of 5-15 with one male, some females and their younger offspring. They are not territorial in the strict sense of the word but they occupy fixed activity zones. They move within the activity zone depending on the availability of food and water. Wherever they find themselves, the dominant bull will defend his females in an area of about 1km^2. An interesting difference between roan and other antelope is that the bull defends the females from other bulls but he does not defend the territory as such. Another interesting point is that the dominant cow takes the lead in herd movements and the dominant bull follows her. The bull remains with the herd at all times.

Order RUMINANTIA
Family BOVIDAE
Subfamily ANTILOPINAE
Tribe HIPPOTRAGINI

Shoulder height m ±143cm, f ±140cm.
Weight m ±230-300kg, f ±220-250kg.
Gestation ±9^{1}/$_2$ months.
Life span ±19 years.
Litter size One.
Habitat Open woodland with areas of tall to medium grass. They avoid short grass.
Food Mainly taller grasses.
Water requirements They drink regularly, needing ±10l / day.
Social structure Gregarious, breeding herds, solitary males and bachelor herds.
Sexual differences Males slightly larger with thicker horns.
Active period Diurnal.
Enemies Lion, leopard and crocodile.
Voice A blowing snort.
Dentition I0/3 C0/1 P3/3 M3/3 = 32

(Hippotragus niger)

Sable antelope

Setswana: Kwalala entsho	**Afrikaans:** Swartwitpens	**German:** Rappenantilope
French: L Hippotrague noir	**Spanish:** Antilope negro	**Italian:** Antilope nera

Did you know?

Body shape and size Sable antelope are large in size and as a result of their raised shoulders and relatively short neck, they show a preference for taller grasses. However, they do also

Order RUMINANTIA
Family BOVIDAE
Subfamily ANTILOPINAE
Tribe HIPPOTRAGINI

Shoulder height m ±140cm, f ±135cm.
Weight m ±200-270kg, f ±180-250kg.
Gestation ±8 months.
Life span ±17 years.
Litter size One.
Habitat Open woodland with tall grass on well-drained soil near water.
Food Medium to tall grasses.
Water requirements They drink regularly, needing ±1l / day.
Social structure Gregarious, territorial breeding herds, bachelor herds and territorial males.
Sexual differences Males are larger, darker with thicker horns.
Active period Day and night.
Enemies Lion, leopard and crocodile.
Voice Snort, bellow and sneeze.
Dentition I0/3 C0/1 P3/3 M3/3 = 32

feed on short grasses, especially in winter.

Habitat The sable antelope, like others in the tribe *Hippotragini* such as roan and oryx, has adapted to survive in areas that cannot support a high biomass. Sable prefer high rainfall areas (±500mm-1 200mm per annum). In Southern Africa, before the influence of man, they were more common on the sourveld grasslands of the highveld and further north (Zimbabwe) in the Miombo woodland.

Social structure They are gregarious, forming herds of ±5-30 individuals, consisting of females with their offspring that may or may not be accompanied by a territorial bull. Females usually remain in the home range where they were born and are hostile to overlapping female herds. This results in very little overlapping of sable territories and accounts for their patchy distribution. A strong rank hierarchy is maintained in the

female herds, the top-ranking female being the leader of the group. She usually grazes apart from the rest of the herd, takes the lead to water and feeding pastures and acts as a sentry for the group. If dominance is disputed by two cows, the herd may break up permanently, but during the dry season there is often temporary, non-aggressive splits to search for suitable habitat. Territorial bulls establish and actively defend territories. The female home ranges may cover three male territories and the male may associate with each group at different times.

±10.5 - 11 cm

48

Lechwe

(Kobus leche)

Setswana: Letsui
French: Le Cobe lechwe
Afrikaans: Basterwaterbok
Spanish: Cobo lichi
German: Litschi-moorantilope
Italian: Palanca

lechwe is the most aquatic antelope. They are completely restricted to seasonally inundated floodplains, where they feed both on floodplain grasses and aquatic plant species. They have virtually eliminated competition by having adapted to a unique habitat called 'water meadow grassland'. This type of aquatic grassland ensures fresh, green grazing throughout the year and consists of semi-aquatic grasses which collapse as the water recedes, forming an ecotone between perennial swamp and the terrestrial communities. The only time that competition occurs with other grazers is when prolonged high flooding forces the lechwes to graze in dryland areas. Lechwes have the additional advantage of being able to feed in water of up to 50cm deep.

Social structure They form loose herd associations that are constantly changing. The only strong bond is between a female and her offspring. The males are territorial but the territories are abandoned when

the water level drops.

Breeding They form a kind of mating ground where a number of males establish themselves in 'hotspots'. The female herds move freely within the mating ground until they are successfully herded.

Order RUMINANTIA
Family BOVIDAE
Subfamily ANTILOPINAE
Tribe REDUNCINI

Shoulder height m ±104cm, f ±97cm.
Weight m ±115kg, f ±80kg.
Gestation ±7-8 months.
Life span ±15 years.
Litter size One.
Habitat Limited to shallow flooded marshes.
Food Water grasses and other floodplain grasses.
Water requirements They are totally water dependent for their habitat and they also drink water.
Social structure Gregarious, breeding herds, male herds and seasonal territorial males.
Sexual differences Only males have horns, and they are much larger than females.
Active period Diurnal.
Enemies Lion, wild dog, cheetah, crocodile.
Voice Whinnying-grunt and a low whistle.
Dentition I0/3 C0/1 P3/3 M3/3 = 32

Did you know?

Body shape The low shoulders facilitate their feeding on short grass species and the powerful back legs enable them to move through the water at speed.

Habitat Next to the sitatunga, the

± 6.5 - 7.5 cm

(Kobus vardonii)

Puku

Setswana: Puku	**Afrikaans:** Poekoe	**German:** Gelbfuss-moorantilope
French: Le Puku	**Spanish:** Pucu	**Italian:** Antilope rojo de agua

Did you know?

Muzzle The puku's muzzle is narrow to allow it to feed selectively.

Coat The hair is quite long, like most of the other 'water antelope', the *Reduncinae*. Compare this to the short coat of the springbok.

Order RUMINANTIA
Family BOVIDAE
Subfamily ANTILOPINAE
Tribe REDUNCINI

Shoulder height m ±81cm, f ±78cm.
Weight m 68-91kg, f 48-80kg.
Gestation ±8 months.
Longevity ±13 year.
Litter size One.
Habitat The 'high water' grassy plains between floodplains and woodland, also depressions.
Food Mainly grass.
Water requirements Completely water dependent.
Social structure Gregarious, breeding herds, territorial males and bachelor herds.
Sexual differences Only males have horns, and they are larger than females.
Active period Diurnal, mainly dusk and dawn.
Enemies Lion, cheetah, leopard, wild dog.
Voice A repeated alarm whistle.
Dentition I0/3 C0/1 P3/3 M3/3 = 32

Hoofs The puku has fairly splayed, elongated, hoofs but much less so than the lechwe. The tracks are 1-2cm longer (±6-7cm), than those of the impala and considerably broader, because they spend more time on wet soils.

Droppings These consist of roundish pellets of which two or three may stick together.

Habitat The grazing and trampling of tall grasses and reeds by elephant, hippo, waterbuck and buffalo in the wake of the receding floodwaters, open up the area for smaller species such as puku, lechwe and reedbuck. Pukus live on grassy areas in the immediate vicinity of rivers. Unlike the lechwe, which follows the receding and rising floods, the puku occupies a 'niche' ('ecological position') intermediate between the wetter area of the floodplain (used mainly by the lechwe) and the drier inland woodland, which is frequented by the waterbuck (Child & von Richter, 1969). This is very well illustrated on the Chobe floodplain (see pg 40). Puku will also venture into poorly drained depressions in woodland.

Social structure They are gregarious, occurring in small herds of about six but occasionally up to 25. The herds are loose associations and individuals come and go. The males are territorial but only during the rut. Some males may hold their territories for longer periods.
Sexually inactive males are allowed in the territory. As with lechwes, females are allowed to move freely across the male territories but a female in estrous will be actively herded by a territorial male.

Waterbuck   (*Kobus ellipsiprymnus*)

Setswana: Letemoga	**Afrikaans:** Waterbok	**German:** Ellipsen-wasserbock
French: Le Cobe à croissant	**Spanish:** Antilope de agua	**Italian:** Antilope d'acqua

Male

Female and young

Did you know?

Glands Antelopes that spend a lot of time in water have glands, known as 'diffuse glands', which are spread over most of their bodies. Their main purpose is to make the skin impermeable to water. The

±8 - 8.5 cm

waterbuck seems to have more glands than other water antelope, rendering their meat unpleasant to predators and humans.

Thermoregulation
The waterbuck has earned its name because of its total dependence on water, more so than cattle or any other antelope. They cope well if there is sufficient water, but under heat stress they have the following restrictions:
Panting and sweating: The only way a waterbuck can cope with high temperatures is to triple its water loss through panting and sweating. An adult waterbuck can loose an amazing 30l of water on a very hot day. To counter the loss, it would have to drink at least 60l. Compare this with the gemsbok that needs only ±3,9l per day under similar conditions. *Inability to reduce urine output:* Large amounts of water is required to dispose of the poisonous urea in the urine, especially for the waterbuck, which feeds on protein-rich grasses. Almost all animals have the ability to concentrate their urine and reduce the volume during a shortage

of water, except the waterbuck. The waterbuck always produces a maximally concentrated urine which means they cannot reduce the volume. At maximum concentrations, their urine is only about half as concentrated as that of the eland (Spinage, 1986).

Order RUMINANTIA
Family BOVIDAE
Subfamily ANTILOPINAE
Tribe REDUNCINI

Shoulder height m ±170cm, f ±130cm.
Weight m ±250-270kg, f ±205-250kg.
Gestation ±9 months.
Life span ±14 years.
Litter size One, seldom two.
Habitat Marginal woodland near rivers and marshes.
Food Medium to tall grass.
Water requirements They are totally dependent on water, needing ±9l / day to survive, but much more under heat stress.
Social structure Gregarious, breeding herds, bachelor herds, territorial males, satellite males.
Sexual differences Only males have horns, and they are larger than females.
Active period Diurnal.
Enemies Lion, leopard, cheetah, wild dog.
Voice Usually silent but they do utter an alarm snort.
Dentition I0/3 C0/1 P3/3 M3/3 = 32

Common reedbuck

(Redunca arundinum)

Setswana: Sebogata	**Afrikaans:** Rietbok	**German:** Grossriedbock
French: Le Cobe des roseaux	**Spanish:** Antilope de la pradera	**Italian:** Antilope redunca prateria

Did you know?

Female

Male

Muzzle The narrow muzzle enables the reedbuck to feed selectively.

Spoor The hooves are elongated to prevent them from sinking into the mud (which is common in their habitat). Their tracks are about 1,5cm longer than those of the similar-sized Impala, which inhabits dry areas.

Habitat Reedbucks have two essential habitat requirements: a permanent supply of water and tall grass cover which they use for hiding and as a food source. They avoid flat, open veld and they will abandon areas where bush encroachment has progressed too far. Burning will also cause them to vacate an area. The tall grass and herbaceous cover provide shelter against predators and the loss of body heat during winter.

Social structure Although about 10 or more reedbuck are occasionally seen together during the winter months, these associations are purely temporary. Reedbucks are not gregarious and form pairs or family parties, but never herds. A pair establishes a territory but there is rarely contact, such as grooming. They may move around in pairs or independently within the territory but they always maintain contact by olfactory and visual means. An unusual occurrence in Reedbuck is that the male offspring may remain with the mother for up to three years. Female offspring tend to leave after two years.

Food They are almost exclusively grazers and are unique in their food choice, especially for their small size, as they prefer coarse grasses that are fibrous, tough and unpalatable to most other species. They seem to favour the tall Turpentine grass (*Cymbopogon excavatus*) and other Thatching grasses, thus limiting competition with most other grazers.

Order RUMINANTIA
Family BOVIDAE
Subfamily ANTILOPINAE
Tribe REDUNCINI

Shoulder height m ±90cm, f ±80cm.
Weight m ±80kg, f ±70kg.
Gestation ±7¹/₂ -8 months.
Life span ±9 years.
Litter size One.
Habitat Vleis, dry floodplains and reedbeds close to water.
Food Tall, fibrous grasses.
Water requirements They need to drink regularly, needing ±3l / day to survive.
Social structure Not gregarious, territorial pairs and temporary, loose groups in winter.
Sexual differences Only males have horns and they are larger.
Active period Cooler parts of the day and at night.
Enemies Leopard, hyaena, cheetah, python.
Voice High-pitched alarm whistle.
Dentition I0/3 C0/1 P3/3 M3/3 = 32

±5 - 6.5 cm

Mountain Reedbuck (*Redunca fulvorufula*)

Setswana: Phele / Mohele	**Afrikaans:** Rooiribbok	**German:** Bergriedbock
French: Le reduca de montagne	**Spanish:** Redunca Montano	**Italian:** Antilope redunca di montagn

Male

Size This is the smallest of the reedbucks, with short and slender horns.

Coat Its overall colour is greyer than that of the common reedbuck. The head and shoulders are more tan in colour and the rest of the body more grey. The coat is pure white below to reflect heat from the ground and from rocks.

Glands It can easily be identified by the black, sub-auricular spot below each ear. This is used for marking their territory.

Social units Since they are strictly sedentary, dispersal is inhibited and they are therefore more prone to extermination during prolonged droughts. The males are territorial and small groups of females (2-3) have home ranges that may overlap with more than one male territory.

Habitat They prefer the eco-tone areas between scrub and grass on mountain slopes. They occur mostly above 1 500m and quite amazingly, they have been observed on the rocky moorland screes of Mount Kilimanjaro (±5 000m above sea level).

Distribution They have a very patchy distribution, occurring in widely separated mountains in southern, eastern and western Africa.

Food Reedbucks in general have evolved to subsist successfully on grasses that are unpalatable or inaccessible to most other antelopes. The common reedbuck makes use of tall grassland near rivers and feeds on coarse thatch-like grasses. The mountain reedbuck ventures onto the steep slopes of mountains. It also feeds on coarse grasses but prefers to feed on them when they are young and tender. Two favourite grasses are Thatching grass (*Hyparrhenia hirta*) and Red Oat grass (*Themeda triandra*). Their low protein/high fibre grass diet, forces them to compensate during the dry season by increasing their food and water intake (Estes, 1991).

Order RUMINANTIA
Family BOVIDAE
Subfamily ANTILOPINAE
Tribe REDUNCINI

Shoulder height m ±75cm, f ±70cm.
Weight m ±30kg, f ±24kg.
Gestation ±8 months.
Life span ±11 years.
Litter size One.
Habitat Ecotones on rocky slopes of hills, mountains and kopjes.
Food Mainly coarse grasses.
Water requirements They are water dependent.
Social structure Gregarious: Small (3-6) breeding herds, territorial males and bachelor herds.
Sexual differences Only males have horns, and they are slightly larger than females.
Active period At dusk and dawn and at night.
Enemies Leopard, brown hyaena, python.
Voice They utter a high-pitched whistle when alarmed.
Dentition I0/3 C0/1 P3/3 M3/3 = 32

Did you know?

±4.5 cm

(Aepyceros melampus)

Impala

Setswana: Phala	**Afrikaans:** Rooibok	**German:** Impala
French: Le Pallah	**Spanish:** Impala	**Italian:** Impala

Female and young

Male

more time in the woodland, which is slightly elevated and drier, but during the dry season they are more commonly found on the floodplains. Their small hoof surface restricts them to soils with good drainage and they will always move to dry ground immediately after drinking, their tracks follow well used trails.

Food If one compares the larger wildebeest (±230kg) to the impala (±60kg), one will presume that the impala will only need about a quarter of the amount of food and a quarter of the time to obtain it. In practice it is quite the opposite. The smaller body size has a faster metabolism and the smaller muzzle takes smaller bites. Also, by being more selective, they require more time to feed. A diet high in protein digests faster and therefore more time is spent feeding than ruminating, which is the opposite for a bulk feeder such as the wildebeest. The impala is thus at a clear disadvantage but it has managed to overcome all the obstacles. Today, the impala is one of the most successful antelope species alive and they have achieved this by resorting to the following: *Intermediate feeders:* They are known as intermediate feeders because they both browse (eat leaves) and graze (eat grass). *Annual grasses:* They thrive on annual grasses. *Split upper lip:* They have a split upper lip, enabling them to feed on very short grasses. *Different strata:* They make use of different feeding strata during different

seasons (eg, grass, leaves, fallen fruit and flowers). *Sedentary:* These feeding habits enable them to remain sedentary (do not migrate).

Territoriality The dominant males are territorial for only a few weeks during the rut. After the rut they remain in a broader home range and intermingle with resident bachelor herds.

Latrines A latrine is initially created by an impala ram in rut, but bachelor herds also tend to use them.

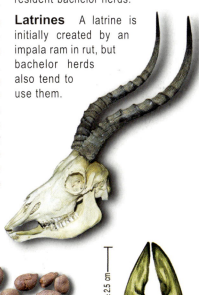

Habitat Impalas are generally referred to as an 'acetone species' which means that they inhabit woodland edges. During the rainy season they spend

Order RUMINANTIA
Family BOVIDAE
Subfamily ANTILOPINAE
Tribe AEPYCEROTINI

Shoulder height m ±90cm, f ±86 cm.
Weight m ±74-82kg, f ±32-52kg.
Gestation ±6,5 months.
Life span ±12 years.
Litter size One.
Habitat From open bushveld to fairly dense riverine forest.
Food Grass and leaves.
Water requirements They need to drink regularly - ±2,5l / day.
Social structure Gregarious, herds of one male with many females and bachelor herds.
Sexual differences Only males have horns and are larger.
Active period Diurnal, but will feed at night.
Enemies Lion, leopard, cheetah, wild dog.
Voice Alarm snort or bark, males utter load roar during rut.
Dentition I0/3 C0/1 P3/3 M3/3 = 32

±2,5 cm

Oribi

(*Ourebia ourebi*)

Setswana: Phuduhudu kgamane	**Afrikaans:** Oorbietjie	**German:** Bleichböckchen
French: L'Ourébie	**Spanish:** Oribi	**Italian:** Dik-dik dik prateria

Female — Male

Did you know?

Body size The oribi is unique in being the only member of the 'dwarf antelopes' or '*neotragines*' that feeds almost exclusively on grass.

Habitat The oribi is only successful under very specific habitat conditions, which explains their patchy distribution. They prefer open grassland or floodplains and do not occur in large stands of tall grass. They prefer mosaic grassland with tall and short grass to provide them with food and cover. Oribis never inhabit woodland or arid areas. They often co-inhabit areas with larger grazers such as elephant, buffalo or even cattle, as these larger animals serve to open up the habitat. This 'opening up' or 'mowing down' is called 'facilitation'. The oribi shows a high preference for recently burnt areas and for low-lying areas where greener pastures are more likely to be found.

Digestive system Their digestive system is primitive, showing signs that they may well have been the first African antelope to have become an 'exclusive' grazer (Hoffman, 1973).

Social structure Oribis are territorial, solitary in monogamous pairs with a tendency to polygyny (one male, several females). Males may associate with two to four females and family groups may join to form groups of up to 12. They are often described as the link between a solitary social structure, as seen among the dwarf antelopes, and a gregarious social structure, as seen in all other antelope.

Territories They have numerous scent glands, the pre-orbital (below the eye) being the most important in their regular scent-marking rituals. They deposit the black secretion onto grasses. If the grass stem is too tall, they will bite it down to a size they can reach. They have communal dung heaps or middens but these do not have any territorial significance.

±4 cm

Order RUMINANTIA
Family BOVIDAE
Subfamily ANTILOPINAE
Tribe ANTILOPINI

Shoulder height m/f ±58cm.
Weight m ±11-17kg, f ±8-20kg.
Gestation ±7 months.
Life span ±13 years.
Litter size One.
Habitat Open floodplains or grass plains with sufficient water.
Food Medium grasses.
Water requirements They usually get enough from their food.
Social structure Solitary, family groups, temporary herds and territorial males (seasonal).
Sexual differences Only males have horns. Females are slightly larger than males.
Active period Diurnal, cooler parts of day.
Enemies Cheetah, leopard, lion, hyaena and wild dog.
Voice Alarm snorting whistle.
Dentition I0/3 C0/1 P3/3 M3/3 = 32

(*Antidorcas marsupialis*) Springbuck

Setswana: Tshepe	**Afrikaans:** Sprinbok	**German:** Springbock
French: Antidorcas	**Spanish:** Gacela Saltarina Bush	**Italian:** Antilope saltante

Female, take note of thin horns

Leon Roodt:

Male, take note of thicker horns

Did you know?

Social structure Springbuck generally occur in small herds, anything from 5-30, which may consist of nursery herds, all-male bachelor herds or even mixed herds. They are very adaptable in their social structure, depending on environmental conditions. Aggregations of thousands of animals take place during favourable periods. Males can usually be seen on the periphery of a mixed herd, but they maintain a safe distance from each other. The adult males drive out the one-year-old males.

Coat The white, thin fur on the ventral and lateral sides is specifically designed for the purpose of reflecting heat from the sun and the ground. The white, long hairs on the rump are known as 'pronk hairs', having the function of insulating the body from heat absorption. These hairs occur in a dorsal skin fold or 'marsupium', earning the springbok the specific name of '*marsupiailis*'. The marsupium can be 'opened' by contracting the skin muscles. This is often done before pronking.

Pronking This is a vertical jump of almost 2m into the air with the back bowed and feet held together, done mostly by the young when they are excited.

Food Springbok are mixed feeders, estimated to eat about 30% grass, 50% trees and shrubs and 20% herbaceous plants. However, the percentage of grass may increase in summer. Their digestive system can cope with plants poisonous to sheep such as Ganna (*Salsola tuberculatiformis*), Bitterkaroo (*Chrysocoma* sp.) and *Geigeria* sp. (Bothma, 1996).

Tolerance to salt They have a much higher tolerance to saline water than other antelope, enabling them to survive near salt lakes. They can survive without surface water, provided that there is ±10% moisture in their food.

Order RUMINANTIA
Family BOVIDAE
Subfamily ANTILOPINAE
Tribe ANTILOPINI

Shoulder height m ±77cm, f ±75cm.
Weight m 33-48kg, f 30-44kg.
Gestation ±6 months.
Life span ±12 years.
Litter size One.
Habitat Dry shrubby veld, open grassland near calcrete pans.
Food Short grass, leaves, shoots and herbs of low, karroid shrubs.
Water requirements They can survive without surface water, requiring only ±1,5l / day.
Social structure Gregarious.
Sexual differences Males are larger and have heavier horns than females.
Active period Diurnal.
Enemies Lion, leopard, cheetah, hyaena, wild dog and black-backed jackal, which kill the young.
Voice A growl-bellow or a whistling snort.
Dentition I0/3 C0/1 P3/3 M3/3 = 32

± 5 - 5.5 cm

Bush duiker *(Sylvicapra grimmia)*

Setswana: Phuti	**Afrikaans:** Duiker	**German:** Kronendücker
French: Le Céphalophe du Cap	**Spanish:** Dik-dik	**Italian:** Dik-dik

Male

Female

Did you know?

Food Duikers are extremely adaptable, both in food and habitat choice. Though principally a browser, eating leaves, shoots and fruit, they also include fresh grass shoots and, surprisingly, a variety of insects and small vertebrates in their diet. This is most unusual for an antelope but an excellent way to increase their protein intake. They eat caterpillars, snails, cockroaches, small rodents and birds. In captivity they have been known to attack poultry and young hares.

±4.5 cm

Water needs As the only savanna-dwelling duiker, the bush duiker has the ability to survive in drier habitats than its forest-dwelling cousins. It gets enough water from its food and even captives seem to ignore water troughs.

Glands Kingdon (1982) reports that duiker lambs, while still lying up, sometimes suck their folded knee. He says that the knee remains a focus of interest in adult interactions and it is possible that there are glands present in the region. They have prominent pre-orbital glands which they use to mark their territory, depositing the secretions on branches, trees and rocks.

Bleating When a young duiker is caught, it bleats very loudly, immediately attracting nearby adults that will rush to save it. Hunters imitate the bleat not only to call up adult duikers, but also to attract leopards and hyaenas.

Tsetse control In the 1960's in Zimbabwe all wild, large mammals were shot as an extreme measure to control the tsetse fly, which feeds on the blood of mammals. Duikers were also shot but, according to Riney (1963) they showed amazing resilience and actually increased during this time. By removing the large herbivores, more food and cover became available for the smaller duiker and they actually multiplied.

Order RUMINANTIA
Family BOVIDAE
Subfamily ANTILOPINAE
Tribe CEPHALOPHINI

Shoulder height m/f ±50cm.
Weight m ±15-21kg, f ±17-25kg.
Gestation ±3 months.
Life span ±10 years.
Litter size One, occasionally two.
Habitat Areas with enough undergrowth or scrub for shade and shelter, avoiding open plains.
Food Leaves, fruit, shoots and flowers, sometimes insects/meat.
Water requirements They get enough moisture from food.
Social structure Usually solitary, forming pairs in the breeding season.
Sexual differences Only males have horns. Females are slightly larger than males.
Active period Nocturnal. Also at dusk and dawn.
Enemies Leopard, lion, wild dog, hyaena and caracal.
Voice Snort and wheezing.
Dentition I0/3 C0/1 P3/3 M3/3 = 32

Steenbok

(Raphicerus campestris)

Setswana: Phuduhudu	**Afrikaans:** Steenbok	**German:** Steinböckchen
French: Le Steenbok	**Spanish:** Antilope rojo	**Italian:** Dik-dik rosso

Female

Male

when urinating, they clear a patch first with the front hoofs and cover it up afterwards. A new site is used each time but they do seem to be scattered around the periphery of the territory to act as markers. The pellets are tiny (±6mm) narrow, pointed on the one side and rounded on the other.

Digestive system They are intermediate feeders, meaning that they both graze and browse. It is impossible for a steenbok to survive on roughage (grass) alone for long periods because of the simplicity of their digestive tract. Unlike roughage feeders, they have a simple rumen which is a blind, s-shaped tubular sac, serving more as a storage chamber than a fermentation chamber. The simple digestive tract of concentrate feeders is designed for rapid fermentation and absorption of protein and fat to cope with their high metabolic rate. However, the steenbok has the ability to alter its stomach structure depending on whether it is predominantly grazing or browsing. When grazing, the microorganisms that break down fibre, multiply rapidly.

Social structure Steenbok pairs establish territories but their movements within the territory is mostly separate. The reason is probably that in their open, exposed habitat it may be to their advantage to disperse,

making them less conspicuous to predators.

Habitat They are well adapted to unstable, transitional conditions in disturbed areas. This explains their abundance along roadsides. The steenbok has proven itself to be very resilient as a species, occurring in high and low rainfall areas.

Did you know?

Faeces The steenbok has a peculiar habit, unique among antelopes, of burying its faecies. The main function is to hide their presence from predators. Even

Order RUMINANTIA
Family BOVIDAE
Subfamily ANTILOPINAE
Tribe ANTILOPINI

Shoulder height m/f ±52cm.
Weight m/f ±9-13kg.
Gestation ±6 months.
Life span ±6 years.
Litter size One, occasionally two.
Habitat Open grassveld (short grass) often in disturbed areas.
Food Leaves and grass.
Water requirements They get enough water from food.
Social structure Solitary or in pairs. Territorial.
Sexual differences Only males have horns. Females are usually heavier than males.
Active period Diurnal, occasionally nocturnal.
Enemies Cheetah, lion, caracal, martial eagle, python.
Voice A soft bleat.
Dentition I0/3 C0/1 P3/3 M3/3 = 32

±3 - 4 cm

Klipspringer   (*Oreotragus oreotragus*)

Setswana: Mokabayane	**Afrikaans:** Klipspringer	**German:** Klippspringer
French: L'Oréotrague	**Spanish:** Dik-dik de montaña	**Italian:** Dik-dik di montagna

Male

Female

but not a very large rumen.

Middens They use communal latrines, which are usually on the periphery of the territory on flat, sandy soil, not on the rocks.

Glands They have prominent pre-orbital glands and they constantly mark grass stalks and rocks.

Parasites The tick, *Ixodes neitze*, is attracted to the pre-orbital exudate of klipspringers which they deposit on plants. When the exudate is washed down by rain, the ticks (which hatch in the ground) climb up and await the return of their klipspringer host (klipspringers tend to mark the same plants repeatedly).

Did you know?

Coat The hairs of the klipspringer are unique among African antelopes in that they are hollow and flattened and not firmly attached to the skin. On the rocky outcrops that klipspringers inhabit, temperatures often reach extremes from frost to 42°C or more. The hollow, flattened hairs are an effective themoregulatory device since air conducts heat and cold slower, preventing heat loss at night and heat gain during the day. The flattened sides provide maximum reflection. In the past the hairs were prized as saddle stuffing. The fact that they come loose easily is a mechanism of defence, preventing a predator to get a good grip.

Eyes The narrow muzzle and the wide eyes, set forward in the skull, give Klipspringers good binocular vision, which is essential to judge distance as they jump from rock to rock.

Hoofs They walk on tiptoe and the hoofs are rubbery, ensuring that they do not slip on the rocks. The track looks like the indentations made by two human fingers.

Digestion They are predominantly (±90%) browsers but they do eat green grass early in summer. As concentrate selectors, they have difficulty digesting cellulose and lignin, both of which occur in grasses. Like other concentrate selectors, they have a large caecum

Order	RUMINANTIA
Family	BOVIDAE
Subfamily	ANTILOPINAE
Tribe	OREOTRAGINI

Height m/f ±50-60cm.
Weight m ±9-12kg, f ±11-16kg.
Gestation ±7-7$\frac{1}{2}$ months.
Life span ±7 years.
Litter size One.
Habitat On or near rocky outcrops and hills.
Food Mainly leaves, fruit, flowers, occasionally fresh grass.
Water requirements Usually get enough from food.
Social structure Territorial. Closely associated monogamous pairs, often with one young.
Sexual differences Only males have horns and females are heavier than males.
Active period Diurnal - early mornings and late afternoons.
Enemies Lion, leopard, python, caracal.
Voice A high-pitched whistle caused by forced expiration.
Dentition I0/3 C0/1 P3/3 M3/3 = 32

C A R N I V O R E S

Order CARNIVORA

Suborder CANIFORMIA

Suborder FELIFORMIA

Family CANIDAE

Wild dog

Bat-eared fox

Cape fox

Side-striped jackal

Black-backed jackal

Family MUSTELIDAE

Subfamily Lutrinae

Cape clawless otter

Subfamily Mustelinae

Striped weasle

Subfamily Mellivorinae

Honey badger

Family FELIDAE

Subfamily Pantherinae

Lion

Leopard

Subfamily Acinonychinae

Cheetah

Subfamily Felinae

Caracal

Serval

African wild cat

Small spotted cat

Family HYAENIDAE

Subfamily Hyaeninae

Spotted hyaena

Brown hyaena

Subfamily Protelinae

Aardwolf

Family VIVERRIDAE

Civet

Small-spotted genet

Large-spotted genet

Family HERPESTIDAE

Banded mongoose

Dwarf mongoose

White-tailed mongoose

Water mongoose

Slender mongoose

C A R N I V O R E S

Name: The name 'carnivore' is derived from the Latin 'caro' = 'flesh' and 'voro' = 'to eat', suggesting that this group contains all the flesh-eaters. This is true but there are a few exceptions, like the civet that is predominantly vegetarian, and the Bat-eared fox and aardwolf that eat mainly termites and larvae.

Suborders: If one refers to pg 34, it is clear that the the carnivores are divided into two major groups or suborders - the *Caniformia* and the *Feliformia*. The former contains mainly the dog-like animals but the *Feliformia* includes the felids, hyaenids, mustelids, vevirrids and herpestidits. One may question why the hyaenas and the aardwolf (family *Hyaenidae*), which are so obviously dog-like, are included in the *Feliformia* (cat-group). The reasons for this are as follows:

Why hyaenas are included with cats: The family *Hyaenidae* had its origins in the *Viverridae* (civet-family) and the hyaenas, not the aardwolf, share with civets an unusual digestive physiology, enabling them to break down complex organic materials such as bone, chitin and semi-poisonous compounds. Another reason for its inclusion in the cat group has to do with the ear bullae (the dome-shaped bones on the underside of the cranium). In the *Caniformia* the ear bullae have no septum to divide the front (anterior) and the back (posterior) parts but in the *Hyaenidae* and other *Feliformia*, such a septum is present. Another difference is the paroccipital process that is attached to the back of the ear bullae in *Feliformia*. In the *Caniformia*, it is independent of the ear bullae.

Dentition: The carnivores retain upper and lower incisors, canines, premolars and molars. In most species the canines are very well developed and elongated for effective killing. The cheetah is an exception with its shorter canines, which are used mainly to suffocate prey instead of severing the spinal cord. Most species in this group also have carnassials. The carnassial shear is the occlusion of the fourth upper premolar and the first lower molar. In some species that do not exclusively eat meat, the molars are better suited for crushing than for shearing. The two most notable exceptions in the carnivore group, are the aardwolf and the bat-eared fox. They are the only two carnivores that eat, almost exclusively, soft-bodies termites and larvae. The bat-eared fox has more teeth than any other non-

marsupial mammal (46-50) and they lack the carnassials. The aardwolf's cheekteeth are reduced to small pegs as they do not masticate their food at all. In both cases the canines are retained and used for self-defence. Most of the large cats have ±30 teeth and most of the dogs have ±42 teeth.

Skull: The cats have shorter skulls and less teeth to accommodate their method of hunting - severing the spinal cord or suffocating. In both cases a shorter skull provides more power. The elongated skulls of the canids afford them a superior sense of smell. The 'scroll' bones in the nasal cavity are larger in dogs. Most carnivores have a thickened ridge at the top of the skull. This is called the sagittal crest and its purpose is to provide firm attachment for the temporalis muscle. In carnivores the coronoid process is very much enlarged and the point of articulation is nearly in line with the tooth row. Both these characteristics add power to the jaw. The mandibular foramen is a transverse groove which limits sideways movement of the lower jaw, such

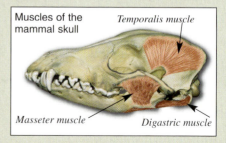

Muscles of the mammal skull — *Temporalis muscle* — *Masseter muscle* — *Digastric muscle*

as is required by herbivores. The temporal muscle of carnivores is their most important facial muscle as it supplies more than half of the pulling force and enables them to tear raw meat apart. The coronoid process provides the lever arm of this muscle and is therefore very large in carnivores. The masseter is less important as it mainly stabilises the articulation.

Senses: Their eyes are set forward in the skull to afford them excellent binocular vision. All carnivores have a *tapetum lucidum* behind the retina. This is a layer of cells that augments the intensity of poor light by reflecting it again through the receptive cells in the retina. This 'mirror' is what causes their eyes to shine in headlights. All members of this animal group have good hearing, but the dogs in particular have an exceptional sense of smell.

(Panthera leo)

Lion

Setswana: Tau	**Afrikaans:** Leeu	**German:** Löwe
French: Le Lion	**Spanish:** León	**Italian:** Leone

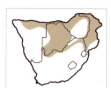

Did you know?

Roaring Lions and leopards are the only cats that can roar. This is caused by an adaptation of the *hyoidean apparatus* or *suspensorium* in the larynx. Read more about this on pg 12.

Order CARNIVORA
Suborder FELIFORMIA
Family FELIDAE
Subfamily PANTHERINAE

Shoulder height m ±110cm, f ±90cm.
Weight m ±180-240kg, f ±120-180kg.
Gestation ±3,5 months.
Life span ±20 years.
Litter size One to five.
Habitat Open woodland, dry floodplains and arid shrubby veld.
Food Large antelope, buffalo, giraffe, also smaller game.
Water requirements They will drink everyday if available but can go without for long.
Social structure Form prides of 5-30 with 1 or 2 dominant males.
Sexual differences Males are larger and have manes.
Active period Nocturnal, sleep during the day, also rest at night.
Enemies Man, hyaenas.
Dentition I3/3 C1/1 P3/2 M1/1 = 30

Food An adult lioness requires ±5kg of meat per day and males ±7kg. They have the ability to go without food for 2-3 days. At a kill they tend to gorge themselves, being able to eat ±20-25% of their body mass in only a few hours (Bothma et.al, 1996). For a 200kg lion that is ±40-50kg of meat. Imagine a grown man of 80kg eating 16-20kg of meat in a few hours! To put this into perspective, this is the equivalent of ±13-16 whole chickens in one meal, calculated at ±1,25kg/ chicken (read more on pg 23). The protein requirement of felids is almost double that of canids. Felids are unable to convert carotene to vitamin A. In zoos they have to be provided with a vitamin A supplement (Fowler et.al., 1986).

Tail Hidden in the tuft is a sharp talon about the size of a dog's claw. It consists of the last small tailbones which are fused.

Induced ovulation A lioness requires multiple matings to induce ovulation (read more on pg 21).

Olfactory communication All cats have sebaceous (fat) glands above the tail, adjacent to the anus, in the genital area, around the mouth and interdigitally. When a lion squirts urine, a musk-smelling secretion from two anal glands between the base of the tail and the anus are mixed with it to leave a message for other pride members or to mark their territory.

±12,5-15,5 cm

Leopard

(*Panthera pardus*)

Setswana: Nkwe	**Afrikaans:** Luiperd	**German:** Leopard
French: Léopard	**Spanish:** Leopardo	**Italian:** Leopardo

Did you know?

Whiskers The whiskers in the leopard are longer and more numerous than in other cats. The whiskers are essential tactile senses to guide them through the thick vegetation that they favour, especially at night when they are most active. The whiskers are linked to a multitude of sensory nerves at their base, which compliments their excellent night vision, stealth and power, making them a lethal predator.

Strength A leopard carries its prey up a vertical tree to secure it, requiring tremendous strength.

The jaw, neck and forearm muscles have to work in unison to get the job done. An adult impala (±40-70kg) is too large for a female leopard to take up a tree but a male can manage young zebra, wildebeest, tsessebe up to ±75kg.

Predation rate Schaller (1972) estimated that a leopard kills slightly more than one animal per week. That adds up to about 60 animals or 1 000-1 200kg of prey per year. This is a very economical rate of predation compared to a cheetah, which may kill twice as much. The reason for this is two-fold. Firstly, the leopard's ability to cache its food in a tree where it is relatively safe from other predators, enables it to feed at intervals over a 3-4 day period. Secondly, leopards are only outranked by the hyaenas when it comes to the ability to feed on rotten meat. The more vulnerable cheetah has to eat its fill in the shortest possible time and is often chased off its kill by other preda-

tors. Also, the cheetah does not eat rotten meat.

Concealing kill Leopards sometime de-gut their prey before taking it up a tree. If not, they let the stomach contents fall to the ground. In both cases they take care to conceal it from other predators by carefully scraping soil and leaves over it.

Order CARNIVORA
Suborder FELIFORMIA
Family FELIDAE
Subfamily PANTHERINAE

Shoulder height m ±65cm, f ±60cm.
Weight m ±20-82kg, f ±17-35kg.
Gestation ±3 months.
Life span ±20 years.
Litter size Two to four.
Habitat In or near thickets, riverine woodland, also arid areas.
Food Prey of up to medium-sized antelope, very opportunistic.
Water requirements They drink regularly.
Social structure Solitary, forming pairs only when mating.
Sexual differences Males are larger than females.
Active period Nocturnal.
Enemies Lion, hyaena, crocodile.
Voice Hoarse cough. Saw-like roar, growl and purr.
Dentition I3/3 C1/1 P3/2 M1/1 = 30

± 9 - 10 cm

(Acinonyx jubatus)

Cheetah

Setswana: Lengau	**Afrikaans:** Jagluiperd	**German:** Gepard
French: Le Guépard	**Spanish:** Guepardo	**Italian:** Ghepardo

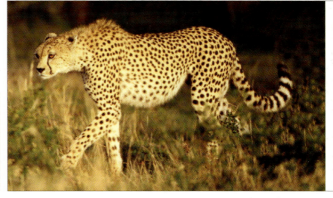

Did you know?

Archaeology Archaeological evidence suggests that the taming of the cheetah dates back to 2 300BC.

Adaptations for speed
The cheetah is the fastest land animal because of certain adaptations: *Legs:* Their legs are longer than in other predators.

Order CARNIVORA
Suborder FELIFORMIA
Family FELIDAE
Subfamily ACINONYCHINAE

Shoulder height m ±86cm, f ±80 cm.
Weight m ±39-60kg, f ±36-48kg.
Gestation ±3 months.
Life span ±12 years.
Litter size One to five.
Habitat Open woodland, floodplains and arid, shrubby grassveld.
Food Smaller antelope, ostrich, warthog.
Water requirements They do drink but can get enough from food.
Social structure Some are solitary, others form pairs, small groups of mother and young or male peers.
Sexual differences Males are heavier than females.
Active period Diurnal, active at sunset and sunrise.

Toes: The toe claws are not retractable like those of other cats, only mildly curved and rather blunt. They are specialised to act like spikes on running shoes to provide grip. *Scapula:* Their scapula lies flat against the deep chest, making it free to rotate in the same plane as the leg, in effect lengthening the leg. *Spine:* The spine also adds to stride length by flexion and extension, whereby the swing of the legs is increased. Hildebrandt (1988) calculated that in theory a cheetah can move at ±10km/h by flexing and extending the spine (without any legs, like a looper worm). *Feet off ground:* The period that the cheetah has all four feet off the ground is twice as much as that of a horse and can be up to 50% of the time, resulting in faster speed - thus almost 'flying' through the air. *Lungs:* Cheetahs have developed a deep chest to accommodate larger lungs. *Strides:* A race horse takes about 2,5 strides/second and the cheetah takes 3,5 strides/ second. *Speed:* A cheetah can run between 85 and 100km/h. Speeds of up to 114km/h have been suggested but 100km/h is a more realistic speed. It is still the fastest land animal, but this speed can only be sustained for relatively short distances.

Endurance Even though it has a caratoid rete system (concurrent heat exchange), which cools the blood going to the brain, cheetahs usually abort the chase after 200-300m and need to rest afterwards. At maximum speed the body temperature may rise to 40,6ºC (105ºF), which will certainly result in death if continued for longer than 500m. At rest their breathing is ±15-20 breaths per minute, going up to 150-160 after a chase (Cawardene, 2007).

± 8,5-11,5 cm

Caracal

(*Felis caracal*)

Setswana: Thwane	**Afrikaans:** Rooikat	**German:** Karakal
French: Le caracal	**Spanish:** Lince	**Italian:** Lince

Caracals can jump over 3m high from a crouching position.

Did you know?

Name The name 'caracal' is presumably derived from the Turkish 'garah-gulak', meaning 'black ear', referring to the black colour behind the ears. They are sometimes wrongly referred to as a lynx.

Ability to jump The caracal is one of the most agile cats, and is a good climber, but its ability to execute vertical jumps defies the norm (see photo above). This ability is essential to catching their main prey, birds, in the air. From a crouched position

±6 cm

they can jump over 3m high. This ability is because of exceptionally powerful hind leg muscles. They often catch their prey in an upside-down position (back to the ground), but they always manage to land on their feet. All animals possess a sense of balance, situated in the inner ear, but in cats it is very specialised, enabling them to recover their upright position faster than any other animal.

History In feudal India the caracal was used for a blood-sport, in which tame caracals were let loose in bird pens. Wagers were laid on which caracal could kill the most number of birds in the shortest period of time (Kingdon, 1989).

Archaeology There is evidence of the domestication of caracals by the Egyptians, as they feature in wall paintings and embalmed bodies of caracals have been recovered in tombs. All cats were sacred in ancient Egypt and were buried in special cat cemeteries.

Social structure They are solitary and territorial. They often forage alone but can be seen in family groups of a mother and her young.

Order CARNIVORA
Suborder FELIFORMIA
Family FELIDAE
Subfamily FELINAE

Shoulder height m ±44 cm, f ±41cm.
Weight m ±9-20kg, f ±4-15kg.
Gestation ±2 months.
Life span ±11 years.
Litter size Two to four.
Habitat Very adaptable, preferring arid areas where grass cover is sparse.
Food Mainly birds, small mammals, reptiles.
Water requirements They can tolerate arid areas and usually get enough water from food.
Social structure Solitary. Pair up only in mating season.
Sexual differences Males are heavier than females.
Active period Mainly nocturnal. Active at dusk and dawn.
Enemies Lion, leopard, hyaena and crocodile.
Voice Purr and chirp like a bird.
Dentition I3/3 C1/1 P3/2 M1/1 = 30

(Felis serval)

Serval

Setswana: Tadi	**Afrikaans:** Tierboskat	**German:** Servalkatze
French: Le Serval	**Spanish:** Serval	**Italian:** Serval

Did you know?

Name The name 'serval' is derived from the Portuguese name for the European lynx 'lobo-cerval'.

Order CARNIVORA
Suborder FELIFORMIA
Family FELIDAE
Subfamily FELINAE

Shoulder height m/f ±60cm.
Weight m ±9-14kg, f ±8-12kg.
Gestation ±2 months.
Life span ±12 years.
Litter size One to four.
Habitat Tall grass, under-bush for cover, close to water.
Food Rodents birds, insects and reptiles.
Water requirements They occur in areas with permanent water and will drink if necessary.
Social structure Solitary. Pairs found mainly in mating season but they often hunt together.
Sexual differences Males are heavier than females.
Active period Nocturnal. Active at dusk and dawn.
Enemies Lion, leopard, hyaena, crocodile.
Voice A high-pitched wail, growl-miauw and a purr when content.
Dentition I3/3 C1/1 P3/2 M1/1= 30

Social structure They are usually solitary but they do have overlapping territories. The male and female associate mainly during mating but may hunt together at other times. A mother and 1-3 young also stay and hunt together.

Droppings The droppings are characteristic in that they are light grey in colour with a powdery white layer, bound together by the hair of mostly rodents. Their droppings occur at random along paths and boundaries and they do not make an effort to conceal them.

Long legs Their long legs are not an adaptation for fast running, but rather for effective mobility in the long grass they favour, giving them height and enabling them to pinpoint sound more accurately, with the help of their enlarged ears. The powerful hindleg muscles enable them to perform spectacular vertical jumps more than 2,5m high. I have seen a pet serval stealing a

defrosting chicken from the top of a full-sized fridge in one effortless scoop and fleeing with it. Their retractable claws are also extremely powerful.

Plucking Of all the cats, servals and caracals are the most skillful pluckers, suggesting that birds form a large part of their diet. In the case of the caracal, birds are probably the main food item but in servals it is second to rodents. They often share a habitat with cane rats and vlei rats, both of which appear in their diet.

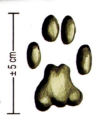

±5 cm

African wild cat *(Felis silvestris lybica)*

Setswana: Tibe	**Afrikaans:** Vaalboskat	**German:** Afrikanische Wildkatze
French: Le Chat sauvage d'Afrique	**Spanish:** Gato montés	**Italian:** Gatto maculato

Did you know?

Domestication Archaeological evidence in Egypt shows that the domestication of the African wild cat goes back to at least 2 000 BC, some archaeologists dating it back to the first dynasty - 3 000 BC. Cats were worshiped and owners mourned their death by shaving their eyebrows. There were annual carnivals in Bubastis or 'the house of Bast'. Bast was the goddess of pleasure and the one who protected humans against disease and evil spirits. To please Bast, bronze statues and mummies of cats were placed in sacred places. By the end of the 19th century, so many cat remains were recovered in Egypt that it was sold as fertiliser - 19 tons were exported to England alone (Morrison-Scott, 1951).

Differences to domestic cats First of all the legs are longer and when they sit up, they achieve a near vertical position, which is impossible for a domesticated cat. The reddish colour behind the ears also distinguishes them. However, there is regular interbreeding where they come into contact with each other.

Social structure They are solitary and strictly territorial. A male range overlaps those of several females. The core of the female's range is aggressively defended. The mother and young can be seen in family groups and the adults only associate during the mating period. The male does not assist with the rearing of the young.

Food They are very powerful killers and can kill prey up to their own size, like hares. They are very adaptable and can overcome the dry period by resorting to invertabrates like spiders and termites.

Cross There are documented cases of African wild cats and servals crossing successfully and although the kittens were premature, they were raised to adulthood (Smithers, 1990).

Order CARNIVORA
Suborder FELIFORMIA
Family FELIDAE
Subfamily FELINAE

Shoulder height m ±65cm, f ±60cm.
Weight m± 4-7kg, f ±3-6kg.
Gestation ±2 months.
Life span ±10 years.
Litter size Two to five.
Habitat In or near thickets, broken country and along rivers.
Food Mainly rodents and birds.
Water requirements They can survive without surface water, getting enough from their food.
Social structure Solitary, pairs in mating season.
Sexual differences Males are larger than females.
Active period Nocturnal.
Enemies Larger cats and eagles.
Voice Hoarse cough, growl, purr.
Dentition I3/3 C1/1 P3/2 M1/1= 30

±3.5 cm

(*Felis nigripes*) Small spotted/Black-footed cat

Setswana: Sebalabolokwane	**German:** Schwarzfußkatze	**Afrikaans:** Klein gekolde kat
French: Le Chat à pieds noirs	**Spanish:** Pequeño gato pintas	**Italian:** Gattino maculatomaculato

Did you know?

Identification This is the smallest of the wild cats, weighing less than 2kg. Compare this to the 3-6kg weight of the African wild cat. It is easy to recognise by its small size, bold spots and relatively short tail.

Name The Small-spotted cat is also known by the common name of Black-footed cat.

Habitat They occur in the driest parts of southern Africa and can be seen in the Kalahari regions of Botswana. They favour areas that offer enough cover such as tall grass clumps or shrubs. In South Africa they occur in the Karoo and the Western Cape.

Food Their food consists mainly of rodents, especially the ones prevalent in the Kalahari such as the Bushveld gerbil (*Tatera* spp.), the Namaqua gerbil (*Gerbillurus paeba*), the Pouched mouse (*Saccostomus campestris*) and the Grey pygmy climbing mouse (*Dendromys melanotis*). They also eat spiders and reptiles such as the spiny agama (*Agama hispida*), which is also common in the Kalahari. This cat can probably be described as a specialised gerbil hunter. In this regard it makes a valuable ecological contribution in controlling gerbil numbers.

Domestication In captivity they show extreme aggression and are almost impossible to tame, quite unlike the African wild cat, which tames relatively easily.

Social structure They are solitary and the only association is between mother and kittens. Male and female only associate during mating. They are nocturnal and very secretive.

Activity period They are strictly nocturnal, emerging about three hours after dark. They are very shy and their secretive lifestyle makes it difficult to observe their behaviour.

Breeding They have an average of 1-3 kittens with a gestation period of little more than two months (±68 days). They have birth peaks in summer, during the rains.

Order CARNIVORA
Suborder FELIFORMIA
Family FELIDAE
Subfamily FELINAE

Shoulder height m±25 cm, f ±20 cm.
Weight m ±1,5kg-1,7kg, f ±1kg-1,4kg.
Gestation ±2 months.
Life span ±10 years.
Litter size One to three young.
Habitat Dry areas with open space, tall grass and shrubs for shelter.
Food Mice, reptiles, insects and birds.
Water requirements They can survive without surface water, getting enough from their food.
Social structure Solitary.
Sexual differences They are very similar.
Active period Nocturnal.
Enemies Lion, leopard and birds of prey.
Voice Growl and spit.
Dentition I3/3 C1/1 P3/2 M1/1 = 30

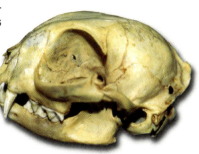

±2.5 cm

Spotted hyaena   *(Crocuta crocuta)*

Setswana: Phiri
French: La Hyène tachetée
Afrikaans: Gevlekte hiëna
Spanish: Hiena moteada
German: Flecken hyäne
Italian: Iena maculata

Did you know?

Social structure They form clans that consist of related females and their offspring. The males disperse at adulthood. It is a matriarchal society in which the males are subordinate to the females - probably an adaptation to inhibit male aggression towards pups. In the hyaena the dominance factor is taken a step further in that the female's genitalia look like that of the male, the testosterone levels in females are sometimes higher and the females are bigger than the males.

Female genitalia The clitoris of the female mimics the penis of the male (pseudo-penis) and is capable of erection. It is elongated and even has a foreskin. The female also has paired swellings in the scrotal area which consist of fibrous, non-functional tissue. It is virtually impossible to sex young hyaenas but once they are adult, the female's teats enlarge and the male's scrotum becomes black and hairless.

Appeasement With animals that have the capability of killing a clan member with one bite, it is important to have appeasement gestures to inhibit aggressive behaviour. This is why, when hyaenas greet, they sniff each other's genital areas to avoid the dangerous side of the body where the teeth are. At the same time they show trust by lifting a leg and exposing their vulnerable underside and genitals.

Bite force The power of a hyaena bite is the most powerful of all mammals for its size - an amazing 800kg/cm². This power enables them to crush a thick bone with relative ease in order to get to the nutritious marrow.

Order CARNIVORA
Suborder FELIFORMIA
Family HYAENIDAE
Subfamily HYAENINAE

Shoulder height m ±75cm, f ±80cm.
Weight m ±65kg, f ±75kg.
Gestation ±3½ months.
Life span ±25 years.
Litter size One to four.
Habitat Open woodland savanna with permanent water.
Food Carrion, fresh meat, skin and bones.
Water requirements They drink and wallow regularly.
Social structure Gregarious, forming matriarchal clans. They usually forage alone.
Sexual differences Females are larger than males.
Active period Mainly nocturnal.
Enemies Lion, crocodile.
Voice "Whoooo-hoop" cries and an excited 'laughing' twitter.
Dentition I3/3 C1/1 P4/3 M1/1 = 34

±2.5 cm

(*Hyaena brunnea*)

Brown hyaena

Setswana: Tlonkana	**Afrikaans:** Bruin Hiëna	**German:** Braune hyäne
French: L'Hyène brune	**Spanish:** Hiena marron	**Italian:** Iena marrone

Did you know?

Social structure The brown hyaena's social structure is very complicated. Since they forage alone they are often mistaken for being solitary. Much like the spotted hyaena, they form clans but their home ranges are much larger - an average of about 300km². They form kinship groups and some of the male and female offspring may remain in the group to maturity. There is provisioning at the den by all members and the females suckle each other's pups (communal suckling). They forage alone and may travel up to 30km in one night, walking at a speed of ±4km/hour.

Caching food They have a strong tendency to cache food, much more so than the Spotted hyaena. They often make more than one caching trip before they actually start feeding. They will carry large pieces of the carcass and hide it under a thick bush to return to it the next day. If the den is close enough, they will carry it there instead. Their high shoulders, long neck, strong jaws and strong neck muscles, equip them to carry large pieces of prey at a time.

Olfactory marking They have two different anal-sac secretions - one is black and one is white. The anal sac is everted and dragged over vegetation. The white secretion is produced by sebaceous glands and the odour lasts longer. The black secretion is produced by apocrine glands and the smell fades faster.

Breeding The females mate with nomadic males and usually not with a clan member. They mate with more than one male. They give birth in a separate den and only return to the communal den after ±3 months. The mother is very attentive to the young but once they are introduced to the communal den, her duties are shared by the other members.

Order CARNIVORA
Suborder FELIFORMIA
Family HYAENIDAE
Subfamily HYAENINAE

Shoulder height m ±79cm; f ±76cm.
Weight m ±35-45kg; f ±28-48kg.
Gestation ±3 months.
Life span ±24 years.
Litter size Two to five.
Habitat Dry open woodland or open shrubby areas for shelter.
Food Carrion, but also birds, reptiles, tubers and melons.
Water requirements They are dependent, eat tubers and melons to survive the driest period.
Social organization Gregarious.
Sexual differences Females are smaller than males .
Active period Mainly nocturnal.
Enemies Lion, leopard.
Dentition I3/3 C1/1 P4/3 M1/1 = 34

±8 cm

Aardwolf   *(Proteles cristatus)*

Setswana: Thuku	**Afrikaans:** Aardwolf	**German:** Erdwolf
French: Le Protèle	**Spanish:** Lobo de tierra	**Italian:** Proteile

salivary glands and emit copious amounts of saliva while feeding. The saliva is essential to start off the digestive process.

Droppings They deposit their droppings in middens. Up to 40% of dirt is ingested with their food. As a result, they have very heavy faeces and Richardson (1990) found that the first defecation after a feed may constitute up to 10% of the body weight - that is ±1kg for a 10kg animal! After the first defecation, they may defecate two or three times more. They make use of communal toilets. One can see the remains of the termites clearly in their faeces.

Did you know?

Preferred termite species
Aardwolfs feed mostly on the snouted termite (*Trinervitermis rhodesiensis)* which, like other termites in the genus, does not possess pigmentation to protect it from the sun and it is thus nocturnal. Some species in the genus *Trinervitermis* forage for only part of the year and live off their harvest for the rest of the time. The aardwolf focuses on those species in which the storage habit is under-developed and

where foraging is required throughout the year. In winter the aardwolf will also feed on the diurnal harvester termite (*Hodotermes mossambicus*).

Skull Its skull is different to that of all other carnivores (meat-eaters) in that it lacks the carnassials and the cheekteeth are reduced, peg-like structures. The canines are well developed and used exclusively for self defence. The palate is very broad to accommodate the broad tongue with which they lick up their food. Their large ears assist them in locating their prey.

Muzzle The muzzle is leathery and naked to protect them against the irritating fluid that the snouted termites (*Trinervitermis* spp) squirt at their enemies in self-defence. The pangolin, which lacks this adaptation, ignores the snouted termite on this account.

Salivary glands Like other termite feeders, they have very large

Order CARNIVORA
Suborder FELIFORMIA
Family HYAENIDAE
Subfamily PROTELINAE

Shoulder height m/f ±50cm.
Weight m/f ±8-13,5kg.
Gestation ±2 months.
Life span ±13 years.
Litter size ±2-3, even 4.
Habitat Dry open country, grass-plains and dry vleis with sufficient termite mounds.
Food Mainly termites but also other invertebrates and larvae.
Water requirements Usually get enough moisture from the termites but will also drink.
Social structure Usually solitary, mother and young.
Sexual differences None.
Active period Nocturnal.
Enemies Lion, leopard, hyaena.
Voice Growl followed by a bark.
Dentition I3/3 C1/1 P3/3 M1/1 = 32

±5.5 cm

(Otocyon megalotis)

Bat-eared fox

Setswana: Tihose	**Afrikaans:** Bakoorvos	**German:** Löffelhund	
French: L'Otocyon	**Spanish:** Zorro con orejas de murcielago	**Italian:** Volpe con orecchie da pippistrello	

Did you know?

Anatomy The 'bat' in 'bat-eared fox' refers to its large bat-like ears, which are held horizontally to the ground to locate underground prey.

Social organisation They form strong pair bonds and often mate for life. They have an average of four young and can be seen in family groups of about six.

Food Because of their physical resemblance to jackals, they are often wrongfully killed by sheep farmers suspecting them of killing lambs. They are in fact totally harmless, eating mainly termites. The bat-eared fox digs for its food by using both sets of claws to dig in the same hole. The holes are characteristically narrow and deep. Other food sources include solifuges, spiders, scorpions, reptiles, frogs, small mice, birds and even wild berries, notably that of the Brandy bush (*Grewia flava*). The poisonous sac of the scorpions is ingested without any apparent harm. It was found by examining stomach contents that the harvester termite (*Hodotermes mossambicus*) is by far their most important prey. Their activity patterns tend to follow the feeding patterns of these termites - shifting gradually from diurnal in winter to nocturnal in summer (Mackie, 1988).

Habitat Since termites thrive in overgrazed veld, the bat-eared fox is also attracted to over-utilised areas, especially in open grassland. Their habitat choice is governed to some extent by the occurrence of the harvester termite (*Hodotermes mossambicus*). The adults have the ability to excavate their own burrows. The burrows are normally about 1m below the soil surface with a chamber of about 45cm high and about 3m long.

Dentition They have more teeth than any other non-marsupial mammal (46-50) but they lack the enlarged fourth upper molar and first lower molar which form the carnassials in other carnivores. The lack of carnassials is the way to distinguish a bat-eared fox skull from that of a jackal. The chopping action of the jaws is extremely fast - up to four or five times per second!

Order CARNIVORA
Suborder CANIFORMIA
Family CANIDAE

Shoulder height m/f ±30cm.
Weight m ±3.4-4.9kg,
f ±3.2-5.3kg.
Gestation ±2 months.
Life span ±12 years.
Litter size Two to six.
Habitat Open areas in dry savanna or overgrazed areas.
Food Mainly termites, also ants, insects, scorpions and larvae.
Water requirements They usually get enough from their food.
Social structure Pairs or family groups. Often mate for life.
Sexual differences Females are slightly heavier than males.
Active period Diurnal and nocturnal.
Enemies Lion, leopard, brown hyaena, spotted hyaena.
Voice Soft "who-who" sound.
Dentition I3/3 C1/1 P4/4
M3-4/4-5 = 46 or 50

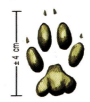

Cape fox

(*Vulpes chama*)

Setswana: Lesie / Mmyane	**Afrikaans:** Silwervos / Silwer jakkals	**German:** Silberschakal
French: Le Renard du Cap	**Spanish:** Zorro del Cabo	**Italian:** Volpe del Capo

Reproduction Not much information is available but some form of sociality is suggested during the raising of the pups. Gestation is 51-52 days. The male does bring food for the female shortly after the birth of the pups and there are sometimes helpers, probably from a previous litter. They only breed once a year during summer.

Food They feed mainly on rodents and birds but will also feed on tubers and cucumbers, especially to obtain water in their arid environment. They do not kill lambs at all but are often killed because farmers think they do. In fact, they have high ecological value in terms of keeping rodent populations down.

Did you know?

Name The Afrikaans name 'Silwervos' refers to the silvery appearance of the coat.

Dentition Although their cheek teeth do have the ability to cut when feeding on mice and birds, they are primarily equipped to deal with invertebrates. Therefore the two molars are broad and adapted for crushing the tough chitin found in beetles.

Habitat They occur in open areas and semi-desert scrub. In Botswana they occur in the Kalahari regions. They dig their own shelters, use old termite mounds or they use ground surface cover.

Social structure They have been described as the most asocial canid, being mainly solitary. The adults do not allogroom or have much contact, except when mating. However, at least one study (Bester, 1982) suggests that they might form pair bonds, but the pair bonds seem to be maintained only when the pups are small. They always forage alone and are mostly nocturnal. They are territorial and defend small core areas around the den, but have bigger home ranges that may overlap with others of the same species.

Order CARNIVORA
Suborder CANIFORMIA
Family CANIDAE

Shoulder height m ±33 cm, f ±33 cm.
Weight m ±2.8 kg, f ±2.5 kg.
Gestation 51-52 days.
Life span ±9 years.
Litter size One to five.
Habitat Open country in drier areas, Kalahari.
Food Insects, reptiles, mice, birds, spiders.
Water requirements They can survive without surface water.
Social structure Solitary or loose pair bonds.
Sexual differences Males are slightly heavier than females.
Active period Mainly nocturnal.
Enemies Leopard, hyaena, python.
Voice High-pitched howl or bark.
Dentition I3/3 C1/1 P4/4 M2/3 = 42

(*Lycaon pictus*) Wild dog / Cape hunting dog

Setswana: Letharelwa	**Afrikaans:** Wildehond	**German:** Hyanenhund
French: Le Cynhyene	**Spanish:** Perro salvaje	**Italian:** Licaone

Did you know?

Social structure Wild dogs form packs of 10-25 animals but only the alpha male and female breed. They are unique among most mammals in that the male offspring remain with the natal pack and the females migrate to join other packs. All members of the pack participate in rearing the young and there is very limited aggression within a pack.

Thermoregulation Their method of hunting requires long-distance chases, which can cause their bodies to overheat. However, they employ a method similar to that used by desert antelope such as gemsbok and

eland. They have the ability to reduce evaporative water loss by allowing their body temperature to rise above the ambient temperature while following their prey over very long distances. By doing this, they actually lose temperature to the environment (Taylor et al., 1971).

Speed Kingdon (1986) reports initial speeds of up to 66km/h, after which they slow down and continue the chase for an average of 2km. This unusual stamina outlasts that of most prey species. Wild dogs have been known to do even longer chases than that.

Regurgitation After a hunt, the adults regurgitate part of their food for the pups and for adults that remained in the den. This is their solution to the problem of feeding the pups at the den. Unlike the hyaena, they are not physically equipped to carry the food for long distances, lacking the strong forequarters, long necks and strong jaws. Wild dogs have instead evolved a capacious stomach in which the food can be stored

temporarily. The hyaena has extremely strong digestive juices that start digestion almost immediately, making it impossible for them to regurgitate food. Wild dogs, on the other hand, often have to travel long distances back to the den and even after a long time lapses, they can still regurgitate, provided that they did not stop to rest. When they rest, their metabolism slows down and the digestive process starts almost immediately, making regurgitation impossible.

Order CARNIVORA
Suborder CANIFORMIA
Family CANIDAE

Shoulder height m/f ±68cm.
Weight m/f ±22-32kg.
Gestation ±2½ months.
Life span ±10 years.
Litter size 7-10, up to 19.
Habitat Open areas and plains in woodlands.
Food Only fresh meat of mostly antelope.
Water requirements They are independent of drinking, getting enough water from food.
Social structure Packs of ±10-25. Only alpha male and female breed.
Sexual differences None.
Active period Diurnal.
Enemies Lion, leopard, hyaena.
Voice Twitter, yelp, bark.
Dentition I3/3 C1/1 P4/4 M2/3 = 42

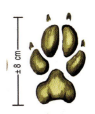

±8 cm

Side-striped jackal   *(Canis adustus)*

Setswana: Rantalaje	**Afrikaans:** Witkwasjakkals	**German:** Streifenschakal
French: Le Chacal à flancs rayés	**Spanish:** Chacal estriado en los flancos	**Italian:** Sciacallo

Did you know?

Habitat Side-striped jackals prefer thickly wooded areas, unlike the Black-backed jackal that occurs in arid, open savanna grassland.

Social unit They form monogamous pairs and family groups.

Food for pups While the pups are very small the male will bring food for the female. Both parents regurgitate food for the pups at first. Once they start to eat solids, the adults carry food to the den for them.

Voice Apart from howling, they also yap and make an owl-like hoot. The San believe they make this hooting sound when closely following a hunting lion and playing with its tail.

Activity Unlike the Black-backed jackal, they are strictly nocturnal. The white tip of the tail hints to this because it makes it easier for them to follow each other at night.

Dens They live in old termite mounds and aardvark holes. The breeding chamber is ±1m under the surface and ±2m from the entrance. There is usually an additional escape entrance.

Disease They suffer from distemper and thousands died during the Kenya epidemic (1906-1907). They also suffer from tick fever caused by the tick *Babesia canis*.

Superstition In East Africa many tribes believe that jackals act as the vehicle for evil spirits sent from the gods. By killing any species of jackal, a blood relationship is formed with all jackals, preventing any evil spirits from reaching them. It is even acceptable if the jackal is run over by a car. Jackals are often associated with death and spirituality. This probably dates back to corpses on ancient battlefields and the jackal's presence as a scavenger.

Order CARNIVORA
Suborder CANIFORMIA
Family CANIDAE

Shoulder height m/f ±38cm.
Weight m ±8-12kg, f ±7-10kg.
Gestation ±2-2¹/₂ months.
Life span ±11 years.
Litter size Two to six.
Habitat Well watered areas in moist woodland.
Food Carrion, wild fruit, small animals, rodents, birds.
Water requirements Usually get enough from their food, also drink.
Social structure Monogamous pairs and family groups.
Sexual differences Males are slightly larger than females.
Active period Nocturnal, also active at dusk and dawn.
Enemies Lion, leopard, hyaena.
Voice Yapping, a 'bwaa' sound and a very typical hoot.
Dentition I3/3 C1/1 P4/4 M2/3 = 42

±5 cm

(Canis mesomelas) **Black-backed jackal**

Setswana: Phokoje	**Afrikaans:** Rooijakkals	**German:** Schabtackenschaka
French: Le Chacal à chabraque	**Spanish:** Chacal con lomo negro	**Italian:** Sciacallo

Photo Leon Roodt

Did you know?

Social bonds The Black-backed jackal is one of the few mammals that mate for life. Both the male and the female take part in rearing the young,

Order CARNIVORA
Suborder CANIFORMIA
Family CANIDAE

Shoulder height m/f ±38cm.
Weight m ±7-11.4kg, f ±6-10kg.
Gestation ±2 months.
Life span ±13 years.
Litter size One to four, sometimes up to nine.
Habitat Most semi-arid habitats but they avoid well-water areas.
Food Carrion, small mammals, birds, fruit.
Water requirements They are water dependent and often drink.
Social structure Forage alone, but live in territorial pairs. They mate for life.
Sexual differences Males are slightly larger than females.
Active period At dusk and dawn, also nocturnal sometimes.
Enemies Lion, leopard, hyaena.
Voice Long drawn-out "nyaaa-aa" sound.
Dentition I3/3 C1/1 P4/4 M2/3 = 42

often with the help of the pups of the previous year. The helpers not only regurgitate food for the pups, but also for the mother. They guard the pups when the parents go out to hunt and play with them, groom them and teach them to hunt. It is not only the African wild dog that that regurgitates food for their pups, in fact, all jackals do it as well. As the pups get older, the parents carry food to them in their mouths. The young follow the parent at about 3,5 months of age. They then abandon the den and sleep in thick underbrush. As the litter of the previous year reach adulthood, they will still be tolerated in the general territory after leaving the family group.

Voice Their most noticeable call is the characteristic howl, which they use as a contact device between family members to advertise their territorial status and to cement family bonds. Family members ignore calls from neighbouring jackals and only respond to members of their own clan.

Activity They may separate during the day but they reassemble late in the afternoon. They forage mostly alone but also in pairs.

Archaeology In ancient Egypt the god Anubis had a jackal head. He was responsible for guiding the dead to the judges and to preside over embalmment. As carrion eaters their presence near death probably resulted in this association. The jackal therefore features very prominently in ancient Egyptian art and hieroglyphics.

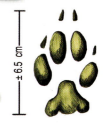

±6.5 cm

Cape clawless otter (*Aonyx capensis*)

Setswana: Kunyana yanoka / Lenyebi	**Afrikaans:** Groot otter	**German:** Fingerotter
French: La Loutre à joues branches	**Spanish:** Nutria del Cabo	**Italian:** Lontra del Capo

Did you know?

Difference between Cape clawless and Spotted-necked otters

Cape clawless otter (*Aonyx capensis*)	Spotted-necked otter (*Lutra maculicollis*)
1. Has nails rather than claws.	1. Claws on all fingers and toes.
2. Eats mainly crabs.	2. Eats mainly fish.
3. Mainly a diver.	3. Mainly a swimmer.
4. Forages in the muddy bottom of the lake, lagoon or river.	4. Forages closer to the surface for swimming fish.
5. Eyes not as well developed.	5. Eyes are bifocal and set more forward in skull.
6. Use fingers to catch prey.	6. Catches fish mainly by mouth.
7. Eat prey in the water.	7. Eats mainly outside water.
8. Less sociable than the Spotted-necked otter.	8. More sociable.

Food The clawless otter searches for its food in the muddy depths of the water and specialises in crabs, rather than fish, like the spotted-necked otter. It also eats frogs and fish. These otters feed in the water by floating on their backs and holding the food in their front feet. Their closest ecological competitor is the Marsh mongoose (*Atilax paludinosus*), but the latter feeds mainly in the shallows.

Adaptation of feet The front foot is specialised for probing and manipulation of food. It is clawless, unwebbed and naked underneath. Most importantly, it has an opposable thumb. There is rough skin on the palms of the front feet to grasp slippery fish and frogs. The dexterity of their hands are quite remarkable. The hindfeet are webbed to enhance swimming.

Dentition The molars are adapted for crushing the hard outer shells of their prey (mainly crabs) and the canines are very well developed.

Play Otters are very intelligent animals. This is evident in their ability to amuse themselves. They play by dropping a pebble in the water and diving it out. They also play 'cat-and'mouse' with fish (Harris, 1968).

Order CARNIVORA
Suborder CANIFORMIA
Family MUSTELIDAE
Subfamily LUTRINAE

Length ±1.25m.
Weight ±10-18kg.
Life span ±15 years.
Litter size One, seldom two.
Habitat Usually in or near permanent water.
Food Frogs, crabs, fish, birds, insects.
Water requirements Dependent on water for its habitat.
Social structure Solitary or in pairs. Territorial.
Sexual differences None.
Active period Diurnal and nocturnal.
Enemies Python, crocodiles.
Voice High-pitched scream, purr, growl.
Dentition I3/3 C1/1 P4/3 M1/2= 36

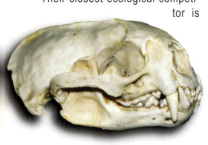

±12.5 cm

(*Ictonyx striatus*)

Striped polecat

Setswana: Nakedi	**Afrikaans:** Stinkmuishond	**German:** Streifeniltis/Zorilla
French: Le Zorille commun	**Spanish:** Mofeta	**Italian:**

Did you know?

Name In East Africa the striped polecat is known as the Zorilla. This is the diminutive of 'zorro', Spanish for 'fox'.

Anal glands The anal glands are not used for scent marking, but purely for self-defence. They are able to squirt to a distance of ±1m. It is not as nauseating as that of a skunk and not as persistent but it does cause burning when it comes into contact with the eyes. Butylmercaptan has been identified as one of the strongest ingredients in the scent glands of mustelids.

Defence When they are threatened, they may stand on their hind legs with the tail held over the body. This aggressive stance and the black and white aposematic warning colours are usually enough of a deterrent. If not, they will present their back to the enemy and their final line of defence will be to actually spray. If they do, the foul smell will usually deter a predator. They may also sham death by lying limp and quickly flipping over if the threat comes too close. During friendly interaction with others of their kind, they present their black underbelly instead of the warning colours.

Food It is more carnivorous than most mongooses, not eating any fruit. They feed mainly on rodents and insects, ignoring toads, crabs and millipedes. Beetle and moth larvae are important food items.

Mating The most amazing thing about polecats is their long copulation. Estes (1984) describes a copulation lasting 106 minutes during which time the male gripped the female's nape and stretched his throat alongside hers. Thrusts were alternated with pauses and the female yapped with increasing frequency.

Protection of pastures They may play a vital role in protecting pastures by regulating the beetle and moth larvae that generally feed on grass roots. In areas where there are no small carnivore predators, entire pastures can be destroyed.

Order CARNIVORA
Suborder CANIFORMIA
Family MUSTELIDAE
Subfamily MUSTELINAE

Shoulder height m ±10,5cm, f ±10cm.
Length: Total 62cm, tail 26cm.
Weight m ±680-1460g; f ±590-880g.
Gestation ±5-6 weeks.
Life span ±8 years.
Litter size One to three.
Habitat All habitats but nowhere common.
Food Insects, mice, reptiles, spiders, scorpions, larvae.
Water requirements They obtain enough water from food.
Social structure Solitary or in pairs or female with young.
Sexual differences Males are larger than females.
Active period Nocturnal.
Enemies Hyaena, owls, black-backed jackal, leopard.
Voice Growl and bark.
Dentition I3/3 C1/1 P3/3 M1/2= 34

±3 cm

Honey badger

(Mellivora capensis)

Setswana: Matshwaane	**Afrikaans:** Ratel	**German:** Honigdachs
French: Le Ratel	**Spanish:** Ratel	**Italian:** Ratel

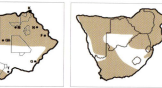

Did you know?

Association with Honey-guide The greater honey-guide bird (*Indicator indicator*) leads the honey badger to the nest by calling continuously and flying from tree to tree until it is near the hive. At this time it falls silent and waits, but does not indicate the exact location of the hive. Only humans and honey badgers respond to these birds. The honeyguide will wait patiently until the badger has finished and then eat the spilled left-overs. Incidentally, the honey-guide is the only bird that can digest wax. They will even eat candle wax.

Anal glands The honeybadger has a pair of anal glands which can exude a very strong odor. Tribal bee farmers in Tanzania maintain that prior to breaking open the nest, the honey badger first turns its back to the nest and fumigates the hive with its strong anal secretions to stun the bees (Kingdon, 1984). There is no scientific basis for this claim yet, but it would be well worth investigating. If this can be proven, it will just add flavour to this intriguing little 'powerhouse' on four legs. Indeed, it has the well-earned reputation of being the toughest and bravest of all African mammals, not hesitating to attack almost any adversary. The aposematic black and white colouring warns potential attackers of its glandular sprays, its lethal jaws and its temperament.

Ear The external ear is visible as a thickened ridge that can close whilst digging to prevent bees from entering the external auditory canal.

Skin The skin is thick and loose and when attacked, they have the ability to manuevre themselves within the loose skin in such a way that they can reverse the attack. The skin is about 6mm thick around the neck. They are not immune to bee stings since dead honey badgers have been found inside hives.

Order CARNIVORA
Suborder CANIFORMIA
Family MUSTELIDAE
Subfamily MELLIVORINAE

Shoulder height m/f ±26cm.
Weight m/f ±8-14$^1/_2$kg.
Gestation ±6 months.
Life span ±24 years.
Litter size Usually two.
Habitat Widespread, except in true deserts.
Food Honey, bee larvae, scorpions, birds, dung beetle larvae.
Water requirements They get enough water from their food but will drink if available.
Social structure Usually solitary but often in pairs.
Sexual differences None.
Active period Mainly nocturnal.
Enemies Lion, leopard, python.
Voice Grunt, growl, bark.
Dentition I3/3 C1/1 P3/3 M1/1 = 32

(Civettictis civetta)   # African civet

Setswana: Tshipalore	**Afrikaans:** Siwetkat	**German:** Afrikanische Zibetkatze
French: La Civette	**Spanish:** Civeta Africana	**Italian:**

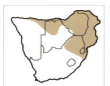

Did you know?

Colour African civets have the black and white aposematic colouring characteristic of animals that possess strong scent glands. However, the civet does not use its glands in defence. In the case of the civet it is probably a form of 'oposematic mimicry', in other words - a bluff.

Territoriality They occupy well-defined territories and the male and female each defend a separate territory, much like leopards. They link up only for the mating period.

Order CARNIVORA
Suborder FELIFORMA
Family VIVERRIDAE

Shoulder height m ±38cm, f ±40cm.
Weight m ±9.5-13.2kg, f ±9.7-20kg.
Gestation ±2 months.
Life span ±12 years.
Litter size Two to four.
Habitat Well-watered areas in woodland with sufficient undergrowth.
Food Insects, fruit, mice, birds, reptiles.
Water requirements They get enough water from their food but will drink if available.
Social structure Solitary.
Sexual differences Females are slightly heavier than males.
Active period Exclusively nocturnal.
Enemies Lion, leopard, hyaena, python.
Voice Low growl, coughing bark.
Dentition I3/3 C1/1 P4/4 M2/2 = 40

Perfume trade The secretion emitted by the anal (perineal) glands of a civet are so copious and durable that these animals have had commercial value since early times. The secretion is known as 'civet'. The musk secretions were not used directly in the perfume industry but as a fixative for flower scents. The civets were held in captivity and they were 'milked' for the secretions by manually pressing both sides of the gland and spooning it out. There is no doubt that the animals were mistreated in the process, especially since the glands do not open into an outside pouch surrounding the rectum but rather into the rectum itself. They were sold along with slaves during the slave trade days, much of which centered around the island of Zanzibar in Tanzania. Today they still occur on the island but it is uncertain if they are indigenous or escapees.

Dung They feed mainly on small vertebrates and invertebrates but fruit, seeds, berries and grass also represent an important part of their diet. They relish Jackalberry (*Diospyros mespiliformis*) fruits. Their mixed diet makes their dung easy to distinguish from other carnivores because there is always plant material present, especially grass strips and seeds. They deposit their dung in a communal toilet, known as a 'civetry'.

±6 cm

Small-spotted genet *(Genetta genetta)*

Setswana: Tshipa	**Afrikaans:** Kleinkolmuskuljaatkat	**German:** Kleinflecken ginsterkatze
French: La Genette vulgàire	**Spanish:** Gineta con pintas pequeñas	**Italian:** Ginetta minore

Did you know?

Family and ancestry Genets belong to the *Viverridae*, the same family as the civet, but genets show more feline behaviour than civets. They miaow, purr and scratchmark like cats but they also glandular mark by adopting a handstand like the Viverrids. Viverrids are considered the most primitive of living carnivores. The earliest fossils date back to the Lower Oligocene. The teeth and skeletons have barely changed in the last 40-50 million years (Estes, 1984).

Glands Like the civet, the genets have small perineal musk glands in addition to the unpleasant secretion of the anal glands. In males it is situated just behind the penis and in females behind the vulva. They are longitudinal and are used for marking. The smell is musky and very persistent. In a zoo situation they emit this smell when under stress.

History The genet is featured in ancient Greek tapestries as a domestic rat-catcher (Bouillant and Fillox, 1955).

Habitat This is the most common genet species in arid areas. They prefer drier areas than the large-spotted genet, but both species occur in the wider Kruger Park region. Their claws are not well adapted for digging, therefore they do not modify holes in which they lie up in. They also do not carry bedding material to the nest. They rely on previously constructed holes.

Hunting They are not as well equipped as the felids to hunt. When hunting, they grab the prey with their sharp claws and give several bites. They do not masticate their food much. The tree rat (*Thallomys paedulcus*) features prominently in their diet. They also eat fruit and seeds.

Order CARNIVORA
Suborder FELIFORMA
Family VIVERRIDAE

Shoulder height m/f ±15cm.
Weight m ±1,5-2,6kg, f ±1,5-2,3kg.
Gestation ±10-11 weeks.
Life span ±13 years.
Litter size Two to four.
Habitat Arid areas such as the Kalahari but also in dry *Acacia* woodland.
Food Insects, mice, small birds, snakes, fruit, seeds and berries.
Water requirements Usually get enough water from their food, will drink if available.
Social structure Usually solitary, mother with young.
Sexual differences None.
Active period Nocturnal.
Enemies Lion, leopard, owl, python.
Voice Spits and growls.
Dentition I3/3 C1/1 P4/4 M2/2= 40

±3 cm

(Genetta tigrina) **Large-spotted genet**

Setswana: Tshipathokolo	**Afrikaans:** Grootkolmuskeljaatkat	**German:** Grossfleckginsterkatze
French: La Genette a grandes taches	**Spanish:** Ginetta con pintas grandes	**Italian:** Ginetta maggjiore

Did you know?

Name In East Africa this species is known as the blotched genet, referring to the larger spots. The word 'large' in its common name therefore refers to the size of the spots and not to the size of its body. They are in fact similar in size. However, one cannot always go by the size of the spots either as there are exceptions. The crest on the back of the small-spotted genet is probably a better way to distinguish the two since this usually lacks in the large-spotted genet. The best is to refer to the differences listed below, but it remains

Order CARNIVORA
Suborder FELIFORMA
Family VIVERRIDAE

Shoulder height m/f ±15cm.
Weight m ±1,5-3,2kg,
 f ±1.4-3kg.
Gestation ±10-11 weeks.
Life span ±13 years.
Litter size Two to five.
Habitat Well-watered areas with sufficient undergrowth.
Food Mice, insects, birds, spiders, crabs, squirrels.
Water requirements Usually get enough water from their food, will drink if available.
Social structure Usually solitary or mother with young.
Sexual differences Males slightly larger.
Active period Nocturnal.
Enemies Lion, leopard, owl, python.
Voice Growl and spit.
Dentition I3/3 C1/1 P4/4 M2/2= 40

Difference between Small-spotted and Large-spotted genets

Small-spotted genet
(Genetta genetta)

1. Dorsal crest more prominent.
2. Spots are smaller and often arranged in rows.
3. It occurs in the drier parts of Africa, including Namibia and the Kalahari, but also occurs in the Kruger Park region.
4. The tail tip is usually white but can also be black.
5. Hair longer, fur coarser.
6. Skull less robust.
7. Legs are longer.

Large-spotted genet
(Genetta tigrina)

1. Dorsal crest mostly absent.
2. Spots are large and form irregular blotches.
3. It occurs in the moister parts of Africa such as swamps (Okavango), riverine forest (Kruger Park), even rain forests.
4. The tail tip is always black.

5. Hair shorter, fur softer.
6. Skull more robust.
7. Legs are shorter.

a tricky business to distinguish the two at night.

Leaping They are very agile climbers and can leap ±3-4m from tree to tree.

Post-natal care The female spends much time with her kittens, licking the genitals and anus to stimulate them to defecate and urinate. She eats the excrement of the kittens (Estes, 1984). Post-natal care may last up to six months. The male only joins the female to

mate and does not assist with the rearing of the young.

±3 cm

Banded mongoose

(*Mungos mungo*)

Setswana: Letoto	**Afrikaans:** Gebande muishond	**German:** Zebramanguste
French: La Mangue rayée	**Spanish:** Mangosta estriade	**Italian:** Mangusta striata

Did you know?

Social structure They form colonies or packs of ±40 with about an equal number of males and females.

Breeding It is interesting to note how they differ from the dwarf mongoose in their breeding. The dwarf mongoose has an alpha breeding pair but in the case of the banded mongoose, all individuals breed. Several males in the pack will mate with the female in estrous. Copulation may last up to 10 minutes (long for such a small animal!).

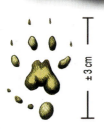

Several females come into estrous at the same time and have synchronised births. The young suckle from any of the females (much in the way that lion cubs do) and all adults help to raise them.

Post-natal care Up to the age of ±5 weeks, at least one adult female remains with the cubs in the den to nurse them, but one or more males may also remain to protect them. The raising of the young is thus a group effort.

Care for invalids Pilsworth (1977) reports that Banded mongooses care for invalids in the pack by giving them preferred access to food and even grooming them and warning them of danger.

Dens They use a den for only a few days or sometimes up to one month but they often return to favourite dens after a while. They make use of abandoned aardvark holes and termite hills. When moving their dens, the adults carry

the young by the scruff of the neck.

Aggression When feeding, they show very little, if any, aggression towards each other. A subordinate will immediately give way to a superior.

Order CARNIVORA
Suborder FELIFORMIA
Family HERPESTIDAE

Shoulder height m/f ±12cm.
Length: Total ±54cm, tail ±20cm.
Weight m ±1,3kg, f ±1,4kg.
Gestation ±8 weeks.
Life span ±8-9 years.
Litter size Two to eight.
Habitat Dense *Acacia* woodland with sufficient undergrowth and riverine woodland.
Food Insects, snails, snakes, lizards, worms, fruit.
Water requirements They usually get enough water from their food, will drink if available.
Social structure Gregarious, live in colonies of 30 or more.
Sexual differences None.
Active period Diurnal.
Enemies Leopard, caracal, raptors.
Voice Twitter and loud chittering sound, very vocal while feeding.
Dentition I3/3 C1/1 P3/3 M2/2 = 36

(Helogale parvula)   # Dwarf mongoose

Setswana: Leswekete	**Afrikaans:** Dwergmuishond	**German:** Zwegmanguste
French: La Mangouste naine	**Spanish:** Mangosta enana	**Italian:** Mangusta nana

Did you know?

fere and prevent other pack members from engaging in sexual activity. Generally he shows no sexual interest in other female members of the pack. But there are exceptions, especially at the end of the female's four day estrous. He may lose interest in her and may also allow other subordinate males to mate with her (Estes, 1984). The alpha female enjoys unchallenged priority while foraging. This also applies to the pups less than three months old and they will often take food out of an adult's mouth. All members help with raising the pups and each age group has a stratified 'job description'.

Social structure The social structure of the dwarf mongoose centres around one mated alpha pair and their offspring. The alpha male and female are the only ones that breed in a pack of ±10-18. The male is only subordinate to the matriarch but he will actively and aggressively inter-

Nannies The adults literally compete with each other to groom and carry the young to gain favour with the alpha pair. When the mother is ready to suckle the young, she lies on her side and the adults carry them to her.

Breeding They breed about four times a year and as soon as a new litter arrives, the previous litter 'falls out of favour'. However, they soon assume their duties in raising the new litter.

Food Apart from insects and reptiles etc, they also eat eggs. They break the shell by throwing it backwards between the hind legs against

a hard object. This method is used by most mongooses with the exception of the water mongoose (*Atilax paludinosus*), which drops the egg from a standing position.

Latrines All members deposit their dung in a communal spot near the den, but this spot is frequently changed. They have separate communal urine deposit spots as well.

Eye The pupil of the eye is horizontal, giving them wider vision towards the back.

Order CARNIVORA
Suborder y FELIFORMIA
Family HERPESTIDAE

Shoulder height m ±5cm, f ±7cm.
Length: Total ±38cm, tail ±17cm.
Weight ±210-340g.
Gestation ±8 weeks.
Life span ± 6 years.
Litter size Two to four.
Habitat Dry woodland with termite hills, fallen logs and detritus.
Food Termites, insects, reptiles, scorpions.
Water requirements Usually get enough water from their food.
Social structure Gregarious, living in colonies of ten or more.
Sexual differences None.
Active period Diurnal.
Enemies Raptors, wild cats, python, jackals.
Voice Twitter, chucks, "perrip" sounds.
Dentition I3/3 C1/1 P3/3 M2/2 = 36

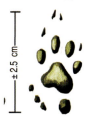

±2.5 cm

White-tailed mongoose (*Ichneumia albicauda*)

Setswana: Leselamotlhaba   **Afrikaans:** Witstertmuishond   **German:** Weisschwanz-manguste
French: La Mangouste à queue blanche   **Spanish:** Mangoste de cola blanco   **Italian:** Mangusta coda bianca

Did you know?

Defence coloration This is one of the largest mongooses, in exceptional cases reaching 5kg and ±1m long. Its large size and its long-haired, white tail sets it apart from other mongooses. Conspicuous white and dark colouring (aposematic colouring), sends out a warning to would-be predators of, in this case, anal gland secretions. The white-tailed mongoose is quite bold and will be totally unconcerned about hyaenas. Its legs are rather long and when the tail hairs are erect, it seems more imposing than it really is. Nevertheless, the bluff seems to work.

Food Judging by its size, one would expect it to feed on large rodents and hares. Although it does eat rodents, it shows a preference for invertebrates, especially harvester termites and dung beetle larvae.

Habitat Its food requirements are very similar to that of the bat-eared fox and the aardwolf, but it prefers moister habitats such as riverine bush and marshes. It covers long distances to forage and is well adapted for long-distance trotting. However, it is not well equipped to dig its own burrow. This is a severe restriction in some areas, causing a rather patchy distribution.

Social structure They are solitary and both the male and the female have home ranges. In the case of the females there may be a few other females and juveniles sharing the range, but they den separately. They do not interact socially but also do not show aggression. A male home range may overlap with several female ranges.

Voice They are highly vocal but their loudest and most unusual call is the dog-like yap or nasal bark. It is very loud and possibly connected with sexual behaviour. The swollen area in the sinus of the skull provides resonance to this call (Kingdon, 1982).

Disease carriers Like most mongooses they carry rabies and they are known as carriers of Rickettsia-borne diseases (Kingdon, 1982).

Order CARNIVORA
Suborder FELIFORMIA
Family HERPESTIDAE

Shoulder height m/f ±22cm.
Length Total ±1,2m, tail ±41cm.
Weight m ±4.5kg, f ±4.1kg.
Gestation ±2 months.
Life span ±11 years.
Litter size One to three.
Habitat Moist savanna with lots of water; along streams, marshes.
Food Insects, termites, larvae, mice, frogs, snakes, birds.
Water requirements They usually get enough water from food.
Social structure Solitary.
Sexual differences Males are slightly heavier than females.
Active period Strictly nocturnal.
Enemies Lion, leopard, owls.
Voice Usually silent. Growl and emit a load, nasal bark.
Dentition I3/3 C1/1 P4/4 M2/2= 40

±5.5 cm

(Atilax paludinosus)   **Water mongoose**

Setswana: Tshagane	**Afrikaans:** Watermuishond	**German:** Wassermanguste
French: La Mangouste des marais	**Spanish:** Mangosta de agua	**Italian:** Mangusta d'acqua

Did you know?

Habitat The marsh mongoose and the sitatunga are two of only a few mammal species that have adapted specifically to the Papyrus swamp habitat, a vegetation type known for its low species diversity. Underneath the floating mats of Papyrus it is very dark and because of the continual dying of the shoots, there is a build-up of organic debris. This causes the water to become low in oxygen and acidic. The water mongoose is not restricted to Papyrus and in the Kruger Park area they occur along rivers.

Social structure They are usually single, except for the

Order CARNIVORA
Suborder y FELIFORMIA
Family HERPESTIDAE

Shoulder height m/f ±15cm.
Length Total ±85cm, tail ±36cm.
Weight m/f ±2.4 - 5kg.
Gestation ±2 months.
Life span ±11 years.
Litter size One to three.
Habitat Always near permanent water.
Food Frogs, spur-toed frogs, crabs, mice.
Water requirements They usually get enough water from their food.
Social structure Solitary.
Sexual differences None.
Active period Active at dawn and dusk.
Enemies Lion, leopard, honey badger, owls.
Voice Growl and explosive bark.
Dentition I3/3 C1/1 P3/3 M2/2 = 36

---

association between mother and young. They are highly territorial.

Food Like the cape clawless otter they prefer freshwater aquatic fauna such as crabs and snails. They also eat reptiles, birds, eggs and insects. Crabs are a favoured food and when feeding on them, they first remove the pincers and then turn them upside down to get to the meat. Upside down crab shells are a good indication of the presence of this species since clawless otters will eat the carapace as well. If the shell is too hard to break, they will stand up and drop it on a hard surface. They also open mussels and eggs in this way. Other mongooses break eggs by throwing them backwards between the hind legs.

Hunting Their underwater hunting is mainly tactile in shallow water, but they also submerge and hunt with open eyes. They systematically work their hands through the mud and water, holding their heads high. The hand

surfaces are smooth and uncalloused to ensure an acute sense of touch.

Coat They have an undercoat that is woolly and about 2cm long. The much coarser overcoat hairs are ±5cm long. Even if they submerge for long periods, the undercoat remains dry.

Paws Their paws lack interdigital webs. The apical (end) bulbs of the digits are not as large as those of the similar-sized white-tailed mongoose.

Ears The hairs in front of the ears prevent water from entering whilst swimming.

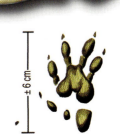

±6 cm

Slender mongoose (*Galerella sanguinea*)

Setswana: Ngano	**Afrikaans:** Swartkwasmuishond	**German:** Rotichneumon
French: La Mangouste rouge	**Spanish:** Mangosta roja	**Italian:** Mangusta snella

Did you know?

Habitat The slender mongoose is one of the most successful and adaptable of the African carnivores. It occurs south of the Sahara from sea-level to 3 600m and can tolerate rainfall from as low as 200mm to as high as 1 400mm per annum.

Teeth They have well developed carnassials, enabling them to feed on tough reptiles and murids (rats and mice).

Manner of feeding When feeding on tough vertebrate food, they feed into a carcass, leaving the skin, tail and feet - a handy 'who-done-it' clue when you find the leftovers of a carcass in the field.

Social structure They are solitary and territorial. Both the males and females establish territories. The male territories often overlap with at least two female territories. It was found that the females will not tolerate another female in her territory but the males may tolerate other males, as long as they do not interfere with their reproductive activities.

Climbing Although they are mostly terrestrial, they are by far the best tree climbers in the mongoose group. They have short, curved claws that enable them to climb and to descend head first, but they are not well-equipped to dig. They have the ability to jump quite high and can easily get over a 1m high obstacle.

Breeding During estrous, the male accompanies the female for about a week. A female can produce several times a year after a ±2 month gestation. The young are born in holes in the ground or in hollow logs.

Order CARNIVORA
Suborder FELIFORMIA
Family HERPESTIDAE

Shoulder height ±9cm.
Length Total ±60cm, tail ±28cm.
Weight m ±450-640g, f ±410-530g.
Gestation ±60 days.
Life span ±8 years.
Litter size One to two.
Habitat Savannah or areas with rocks and tree trunks for shelter.
Food Termites, insects, lizards, bird eggs, larvae, snakes.
Water requirements They usually get enough water from their food.
Social structure Solitary.
Sexual differences Males are slightly larger than females.
Active period Diurnal.
Enemies Leopard, wild cats, jackal, civet.
Voice Spitting and caterwauling.
Dentition I3/3 C1/1 P4/3 M2/2 = 38

±3 cm

(Cynictus penicillata) **Yellow mongoose**

Setswana: Moswe	**Afrikaans:** Witkwasmuishond	**German:** Fuchsmanguste
French: Mangouste faure	**Spanish:** Mangosta amarilla	**Italian:** Manguste gialla

Did you know?

Habitat The Yellow mongoose prefers open habitats in sandy soil, but also occurs in savanna woodland, *Acacia* veld and even on floodplains. In Botswana they are most common in the southern Kalahari (Kgalagadi Transfrontier Park) but also occur in the Makgadikgadi pans area and in Savute (Chobe National Park).

Social structure This is a social species and may occur in family groups or in pairs. They mostly form small colonies of about 20 animals Some older individuals may live separately but will still maintain friendly contact with the group. They have a clear rank hierarchy. Each group

Order CARNIVORA
Suborder FELIFORMIA
Family HERPESTIDAE

Shoulder height m/f ±10cm.
Weight m/f ±480-800g.
Gestation ±8 weeks.
Life span ±7 years.
Litter size Two to five young.
Habitat Open dry scrubby areas and grassland.
Food and Insects, mice, reptiles, birds.
Water requirements Get enough water from food, will also drink.
Social structure Gregarious, colonies up to 20 members
Sexual differences None
Active period Diurnal.
Enemies Wild cats, raptors, hyaena, jackal.
Voice Growl and hiss.
Dentition I3/3 C1/1 P4/4 M2/2 = 40

has a breeding alpha male and female. All colony members submit to the alpha male and female but in general the young are more dominant over other adults. The very old mongooses are thus the lowest in rank. They are territorial and the alpha male will regularly patrol the boundaries of the territory. The male usually marks the boundaries with anal sac secretions in the mornings before going out to feed. The alpha male also marks each member of his colony before they all disperse to forage alone.

Foraging Colony members forage individually, but they may be in sight of each other if there is an over-abundance of food.

Warrens They occupy extensive warrens with numerous entrances similar to that of the suricate. In fact, they may even share the warren with the suricate and the ground squirrel, both of which are also communal animals.

This is an interesting situation because the suricate and yellow mongoose are predators, but they seldom attack the ground squirrels.

Breeding Births take place early in the rains (±November). Copulations can be long - from 30-45 minutes, much like the White-tailed mongoose, which is even longer! Subordinate females sometimes mate with different males but this does not result in pregnancies as far as can be established.

±3 cm

Suricate

(*Suricata suricata*)

Setswana: Lejara	**Afrikaans:** Swartkwasmuishond	**German:** Rotichneumon
French: La Suricate	**Spanish:**	**Italian:**

Kalahari.

Warrens The warrens can be from ±5-25m in diameter. There may be as many as 50-80 entrances in a large warren. The warrens consist of tunnels with an occasional chamber of ±30cm high where they huddle together to sleep. They can excavate their own warrens but they often prefer to occupy existing burrows prepared by ground squirrels and/or yellow mongooses, with which they sometimes share the same warren.

Temperature regulation The Kalahari is known for extremes in temperature - very hot days and very cold nights. The Suricate avoids these climatic extremes by using its underground shelters both to get warm and cold. Estes (1984) reports that the minimum and maximum inside a warren was ±10°C and 23°C while outside temperatures varied from ±-4°C and ±38,5°C. The thinly-haired belly of the suricate is exposed to the sun in the morning to warm up. During the heat of the day they lie flat on a moist, cool soil surface to cool down.

Social structure They are highly sociable and (as with the banded mongoose) there are several breeding males and females and not only an

alpha pair (as is the case with the dwarf mongoose and the yellow mongoose). They form packs of about 10-30. There is no sign of a linear hierarchy and there is very little aggression within the pack. However, they do band together to aggressively deter predators and rivals. The largest male is usually the most aggressive in such encounters.

Breeding In captivity they can produce continuously. In nature, climatic conditions limit them to breeding during summer but they may still have up to three litters of about three pups each.

Did you know?

Habitat Of all the mongooses, suricates live in the most arid conditions and also in the most open environment. In Botswana they occur in the

---

Order CARNIVORA
Suborder y FELIFORMIA
Family HERPESTIDAE

Shoulder height m/f ±9cm.
Length m/f ±45-65cm, including tail.
Weight m ±620-730g,
f 680-950g.
Gestation 10 - 11 weeks.
Life span ±8 years.
Litter size Two to five.
Habitat Open areas in Kalahari. scrub, on hard calcareous soil.
Food Worms, insects, larvae, mice, spiders.
Water requirements Obtain enough moisture from their food.
Social structure Live in colonies up to 20 animals.
Sexual differences Females are slightly larger than males.
Active period Exclusively diurnal.
Enemies Leopard, jackal, hyaena, birds of prey.
Voice A sharp, loud alarm bark.
Dentition I3/3 C1/1 P3/3 M2/2 = 36

±3.5 cm

Order PRIMATA

Suborder HAPLORHINI

Superfamily CERCOPITHECOIDEA

Family Cercopithecidae

Chacma baboon

Vervet monkey

Suborder CANIFORMIA

Superfamily LORISOIDEA

Family Galagidae

Greater galago

Lesser galago

This order include the great apes, monkeys, baboons, bushbabies and humans and they all share the following: They have long backs, short, flexible necks, five-digit hands and feet, forward-oriented eyes for binocular vision and forearms that are linked to the chest by a collarbone (clavicle). In other groups, especially those that need speed, the clavicle is rudimentary or absent.

This group consists of the Scaly ant-eaters. The scales are cornified extrusions of the outer skin. They have long tongues and long, muscular tails, enabling them to roll into a ball as a defence mechanism. Their stomachs are muscular and work like a bird's gizzard.

Order PHOLIDOTA

Family Manidae

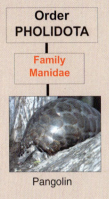

Pangolin

Hyraxes have two enlarged upper incisors that grow throughout life. This is about the only thing the hyrax still shares with elephants. There is evidence that they shared an early fossil lineage with elephants. Their long gestation (8 months) is evidence that they were much larger earlier in their evolution.

Order HYRACOIDEA

Family Procaviidae

Rock hyrax

Order TUBULIDENTATA

Family Orycteropodidae

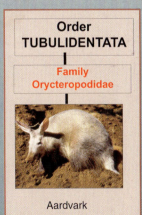

Aardvark

The aardvark is the only member of this order. Its teeth consist of densely packed tubules surrounded by dentine. The teeth lack enamel.

Order LAGOMORPHA

Family Leporidae

Scrub hare

Cape hare

Their teeth superficially resemble rodent teeth with chisel-like, paired incisors, but unlike rodents, their incisors are wholly sheathed in enamel and the upper pair has a second pair of tiny peg teeth behind it. Lagomorphs can survive on coarse plant material because they practice coprophagy (they re-ingest their excreted pellets).

Chacma baboon

(Papio ursinus)

Setswana: Tshwene	**Afrikaans:** Bobbejaan	**German:** Steppenpavian
French: Le Babouin	**Spanish:** Babuino	**Italian:** Babbuino

Did you know?

Social structure Chacma baboons form large troops of 20 to 200, but usually ±45-60. The females make up the stable core of the group as they remain in the natal group or an offshoot of the natal group for their whole lives. Males emigrate to other groups and may link up with a number of groups in their life time.

Rank dominance A very strict hierarchy exists between the adult females and their young. Within the troop there is a number of female 'kinship' groups, each of which belongs to a certain rank. The young inherit the rank of their mother. Therefore, even adult females of lower rank are subordinate to the offspring of the dominant kinship matriarch. Young males remain in this group until they are ±4 years old. At this time they become mature and then become dominant over all females, and even the males of lower ranking females.

Godfathers The males that often associate with a specific female also take on a godfather role with her offspring, even if they are not his own (very often they are his own). Within the troop, each youngster thus has a male caretaker that will defend it during a squabble.

Lack of sexual aggression There is very little sexual aggression in a baboon troop and

it is not only the dominant males that mate. Females show a preference to mate with males that she regularly associates with. Each female may have 1-3 such favourites. They often forage and root in close proximity. Other, more dominant males, do not seem to mind this, as they themselves have a core group to which they belong.

Dead infants A mother will carry a dead infant for days on end and will show confusion and frustration with the limp body. It is heartbreaking to witness.

Order PRIMATA
Suborder HAPLORHINI
Superfamily CERCOPITHECOIDEA
Family CERCOPITHECIDAE

Shoulder height m ± 65cm, f ± 50cm (when standing on all fours).
Length m ±155cm, f ±125cm.
Weight m ±20-44kg, f ±14-17kg.
Gestation ±6 months.
Life span ±18 years.
Litter size One, seldom two.
Habitat Prefer mountainous and well-wooded areas.
Food Opportunistic omnivore. Wild fruit, berries, insects, meat.
Water requirements Water dependent, drink daily.
Social structure Form troops of up to 70 and have a distinct hierarchy.
Sexual differences Males are larger and more aggressive.
Active period Diurnal.
Enemies Leopard and lion.
Voice Growl, bark, "bawchom", screaming.
Dentition I2/2 C1/1 P2/2 M3/3 = 32

±15 cm

±8.5 cm

(Cercopithecus aethiops)   **Vervet monkey**

Setswana: Kgabo	**Afrikaans:** Blouaap	**German:** Blaue Affe
French: Le Grivet/Senge	**Spanish:** Mono	**Italian:** Sciossia zanzibarina

Did you know?

Anatomy The vervet monkey's limb proportions are not specialised for either an arboreal or a terrestrial lifestyle, but their intermediate status gives them the advantage of being adaptable to a wide variety of habitats and certainly contributes to their success as a species.

Social structure Their social structure is very complicated - in many instances like that of baboons. It consists of a troop of 20-40 animals with a hierarchy of kinships within the troop. The members of each family group feed and sleep together. It is also a female-bonded society where the females remain in the group and the males emigrate to other groups at maturity. Similar to baboons, the mother's rank predetermines that of her offspring. Interestingly, subordinate members of the group vie with one another to groom dominant individuals, thereby improving their own rank if they are accepted by the more dominant individual. In other words, it is not what you know, but who you know! Sounds familiar, doesn't it?

Order PRIMATA
Suborder HAPLORHINI
Superfamily CERCOPITHECOIDEA
Family CERCOPITHECIDAE

Shoulder height ±25-30cm.
Length Body ±50cm, tail ±55cm.
Weight m ±3.8-8kg,
f ±3.4-5.2kg.
Gestation ±7 months.
Life span ±12 years.
Litter size One, seldom two.
Habitat Woodland, river banks, often close to human habitation.
Food Wild fruit, flowers, seeds, insects, birds, eggs.
Water requirements Water dependent.
Social organization Gregarious, troops up to 20.
Sexual differences Males are larger.
Active period Diurnal.
Enemies Leopard, lion, caracal, crowned eagle.
Voice Chatterring and high pitched screams.
Dentition I2/2 C1/1 P2/2 M3/3 = 32

brothers and to avoid unnecessary danger, they often move to troops where an older male relative has already established himself. Looking at the teeth in the skull below, that makes perfect sense!

Communication Research has shown that they have at least 60 gestures and 36 distinct sounds that play a role in communication. They have shown the ability to recognise individual troop members and even neighbouring troop members totally by sound when recordings were played to them.

Emigration of males When males emigrate, they usually do so in the company of peers or

± 9.5 cm

Thick-tailed bushbaby (*Otolemur crassicaudatus*)

Setswana: Ramogwele	**Afrikaans:** Bosnagaap	**German:** Riesengalago
French: Galago à queue épaisse	**Spanish:** Galago de cola gruesa	**Italian:**

Did you know?

Teeth The canine teeth in the upper jaw are well developed and sharply pointed. The incisor teeth in the bottom jaw are long and thin and pointed forward and the canine teeth look like incisors. The incisors are mainly used like a comb for grooming.

Feet/hands These bushbabies have five digits on their hands and feet with human-like nails. The second digit on the hind foot has a claw of ±7mm across the curve that is used for grooming. The thumb and big toe are opposable, enabling them to grasp branches and insects.

Scent marking They have a longitudinal patch on the middle of the chest which is hairless and contains apocrine glands. These glands secrete a yellow, oily substance. This is rubbed against trees along their usual routes. The greater and the lesser bushbaby also employ urine washing (see Lesser bushbaby, pg 94 for more details).

Habitat They are associated with the eastern higher rainfall areas of Southern Africa and are associated with well-developed woodland or riverine forest. The lesser bushbaby is associated with more open savanna.

Food Both bushbabies have specialised in feeding on gum exuded by trees. This is a food source not used by many animals, with the exception of arboreal rodents such as the tree rat (*Thallomys paedulcus*). They also feed on seeds, fruit, flowers and insects.

Catching insects Bush-babies are specifically adapted to catch the fast-moving insects. This is achieved by a superior sense of hearing, eyesight and hand-eye coordination. They capture their prey with a rapid grab in which all the fingers converge on the palm. They cannot move their fingers separately like monkeys and baboons can.

Social structure They live together in family groups consisting of a male, female and their offspring. The larger males often control more than one female range.

Order PRIMATA
Suborder STREPSIRHINI
Superfamily LORISOIDEA
Family GALAGIDAE

Length Body ±35cm, tail ±40cm.
Weight m/f ±1,1kg.
Gestation ±4 months.
Life span ±12 years.
Litter size Two.
Habitat Riverine forests, mountains, coastal forests, woodland.
Food Acacia gums, fruit, insects, larvae, mice, spiders, birds.
Water requirements Usually get enough water from their food.
Social structure Gregarious, family groups of male, female and young.
Sexual differences Males are a little larger than females.
Active period Nocturnal.
Enemies Leopard, giant eagle owl.
Voice Very vocal - ominous, hoarse wailing or rattling alarm.
Dentition I2/2 C1/1 P3/3 M3/3 = 36

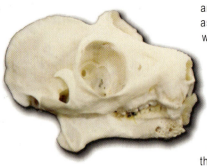

±3.5 cm

(*Galago maholi*)   Lesser bushbaby

Setswana: Mogwele	**Afrikaans:** Nagapie	**German:** Steppengalago
French: Galago du Sénégal	**Spanish:** Galago del Senegal	**Italian:**

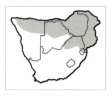

Did you know?

Vision Unlike most animals, bushbabies cannot move their eyes from side to side, mostly because the eyes are so enlarged that they occupy the socket completely, leaving no room for muscle attachment. They do compensate by having bulging eyes that give them a ±250° stationary field of vision. That is more than 50° greater than man. They also have the ability to move their heads through 180°, enabling them to see behind them without moving the body. They have a well-developed *tapetum lucidum* (mirror-like layer of cells at the back of the eye, which enhances night vision). It is this layer that caus-es their eyes to shine so brightly in the headlights at night.

Grooming Bushbabies groom mostly with their teeth and the second digit on the hind foot. Their lower canines have been adapted to look like incisors to form a 'comb' to groom their fur. Interestingly, they have a kind of secondary tongue just below the lower tooth row, which is employed to remove the hairs caught in the teeth while grooming.

Urine washing Urine washing is when they urinate on their front paws and dab it on their hind paws. The main purpose of this activity is for scent marking rather than for improving grip, since they do it more frequently around their nesting site.

Jumping They can jump ±2,25m vertically (Hall-Craggs, 1965) from a standing position. This superior performance can be explained by the larger muscle mass of the hind legs and the proportions of the limbs. Their jumping muscles comprise 10% of their body mass (Alexander, 1968). This is about twice as much as in man. They have been recorded to do 5,5m horizontal jumps and can drop anything from 3m to 6m.

Breeding They reproduce twice a year - first during the early wet season (October - November) and then during the late wet season (March). The gestation is exceptionally long for such a small animal - 121 days (±4 months). The female comes into estrous straight after the first birth but not after the second.

Order PRIMATA
Suborder STREPSIRHINI
Superfamily LORISOIDEA
Family GALAGIDAE

Length Body ±17cm, tail ±25cm.
Weight m ±155g, f ±150g.
Gestation ±4 months.
Life span ±10 years.
Litter size One to two.
Habitat Acacia woodland.
Food Gum, grasshoppers, moths, spiders.
Water requirements They usually get enough from their food.
Social organization Gregarious, territorial.
Sexual differences None.
Active period Nocturnal.
Enemies Owls, genets, leopard.
Voice A "chak-chak" and growl sound, which becomes louder.
Dentition I2/2 C1/1 P3/3 M3/3 = 36

±3 cm

Pangolin

(*Manis temminckii*)

Setswana: Kgaga	**Afrikaans:** Ietermagog	**German:** Steppen-schuppentier
French: Pangolin de Temminck	**Spanish:** Pangolin	**Italian:** Pangolino

Did you know?

Skull The skull of the pangolin is very simple in shape (pear-shaped) and there are no teeth. On the upper jaw is a narrow ridge of bone where the teeth would have been. The lower jaw bone consists of a simple, fragile, v-shaped structure which is not developed enough to play any part in the chewing of food.

Tongue The tongue is long and sticky. It is inserted deep into the cavities of ant nests to gather the ants. When the pangolin is not feeding, the tongue is drawn into a sheath well into the chest cavity where it is attached to the breast-bone (read more under 'skeleton').

Skeleton The xiphisternum (the cartilaginous process forming the lowermost part of the breastbone or sternum) is greatly elongated in this species. It follows the lower abdominal wall and bends upwards behind the abdominal cavity to the region of the kidneys. Its function is to provide a base for the elongated, sticky tongue.

Food Pangolins feed mainly on formicid ants, particularly their larvae and pupae. Species that they favour include *Anoplolepis custodiens* and *Paltothyreus tarsatus*. They do occasionally eat termites. They open up the nests with their front claws.

Claws The front claws are up to 4,5cm long and are perfect tools to open up ant nests.

Stomach The function of chewing has been taken over by a complex stomach. The food is ground up by the powerful stomach muscles. The large amount of soil that is ingested probably helps with the grinding process. The capacious stomach has much the same function as the gizzard of a bird, in which the usual mucous membrane lining is replaced by a horny epithelium.

Salivary glands The pangolin has hugely enlarged salivary glands on the sides of the head, which extend almost to the shoulders. Copious amounts of saliva is essential for proper digestion as no mastication takes place at all.

Scent glands Around the anus are a number of bean-shaped glands. When stressed the pangolin emits a vile-smelling fluid spray.

Order PHOLIDOTA
Family MANIDAE

Length Body ±50cm; tail ±40cm.
Weight m/f ±5-18kg.
Gestation ±4½ months.
Life span ±12 years.
Litter size One.
Habitat Very adaptable, requiring mainly cover and ants.
Food Mainly ants, also termites.
Water requirements They get enough moisture from their food.
Social organization Solitary or mother & baby.
Sexual differences None.
Active period Mainly night.
Enemies Lion, leopard, hyaena.
Voice Audible snuffling when feeding and a hiss when rolled up into a ball.
Dentition I0/0 C0/0 P0/0 M0/0 = 0

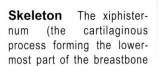

(Orycteropus afer)   Aardvark

Setswana: Thakadu	**Afrikaans:** Erdvark	**German:** Erdferkel
French: Le Fourmillier	**Spanish:** Oso hormiguero	**Italian:**

Did you know?

Dentition The family name 'Tubulidentata' means 'tubule-toothed' and refers to the six-sided structures that surround tiny tubular pulp cavities. It seems totally superfluous for aardvarks to have teeth at all as they do not masticate their food. They lack incisors and canine teeth.

Order TUBULIDENTATA
Family ORYCTEROPODIDAE

Height m/f ±60-65cm.
Weight m ±45-65kg, f ±40-58kg.
Gestation ±7 months.
Life span ±10 years.
Litter size One.
Habitat They prefer soils that are not very compacted, where termites occur.
Food Mainly mound-building termites, but also ants.
Water requirements They obtain enough water from their food, will occasionally drink.
Social structure Solitary, only form pairs during mating.
Sexual differences Males are larger than females.
Active period Nocturnal.
Enemies Lion, leopard, hyaena.
Voice Grunt and sniff.
Dentition I0/0 C0/0 P2/2 M3/3 = 20

Sense of smell They have an acute sense of smell, enabling them to locate their subterranean food. This is evident in the convoluted (rolled upon itself) structure of the epithelium within the nasal cavity. The latter is also referred to as 'turbinal surfaces', having the function of processing the olfactory stimuli. In the aardvark this area is enlarged and is visible as a swelling in the central region of the skull. The olfactory bulbs, which are situated in the front part of the brain, are exceptionally large in the aardvark.

Food Aardvarks feed on both ants and termites, with termites eaten mainly during the rainy season and ants during the dry season. The reason is that mound-building termites are much less active during winter and the aardvark is forced to resort to ants. When in search of prey, it walks with its nose close to the ground, uttering a load sniff. They also feed on the pupae of dung beetles, which lay buried 30cm or 40cm below the sur-face in dung pellets. Wild melons are also eaten and contribute moisture to their diet.

Stomach The stomach is markedly constricted and muscled in the pylorus region (opening to the small intestine). The aardvark is equipped with large salivary glands and together with the muscular movement in the pyloric area of the stomach, digestion is very efficient. The stomach acts much like a bird's gizzard, grinding the food - an action that takes over the function of teeth.

±11 cm

Scrub hare

(*Lepus saxatilis*)

Setswana: Mutlwa
French: Le Liévre des buissons
Afrikaans: Kolhaas
Spanish: Liebre del Cabo
German: Buschhaase
Italian: Lepre da cespuqlio

Did you know?

Difference between the Scrub hare and Cape hare

Lepus saxatilis Scrub hare	*Lepus capensis* Cape hare
1. Scrub hare is slightly larger.	1. Cape hare slightly smaller.
2. They occur in woodland and scrubland, not in desert and open grassland.	2. They prefer open grassland and salt pan areas. Do not occur in woodland.
3. They mainly graze.	3. They browse and graze.
4. Chest and abdomen are completely white without an ochre band separating the white underparts and the rest.	4. Chest and abdomen are either completely pinkish-buff or white in the centre with a pinkish-yellow band between the underparts and the rest.

Social structure They are solitary and non-territorial. When in estrous, the female may be accompanied by one or more males.

Dens They lie up in a form, well concealed under bushes and in grass, even when having their young. They lie with their ears flat against the body.

Digestion See pg 68.

Hares and rabbits The differences between hares and rabbits are based on the fact that rabbits burrow and hares do not. Hares need to be well camouflaged, extremely agile and fast to escape predation, therefore the hind legs tend to be longer than the front ones. They also have a broader air passage to facilitate a greater oxygen requirement when escaping predation. Since hares have their young in the open with only the protection of bushes, the young are precocial, meaning they are well-developed at birth. Rabbits are more conspicuous, not fast, do not have a broad trachea or well-developed hind legs, and they have altricial young.

Young Since the young of hares are so vulnerable in the open or under bushes, they have virtually no smell and even dogs have been known to walk almost right over them without detection.

Order LAGOMORPHA
Family LEPORIDAE

Length ±60cm long.
Weight m ±1,4-3,8kg, f ±1,6-4,5kg.
Gestation ±5 weeks.
Litter size ±1-3.
Life span ±5 years.
Habitat Open, dry woodland or shrubland. They lie up under shrubs and do not have underground dens.
Food Short grasses.
Water requirements Obtain enough water from their food.
Social structure Solitary or mother and young.
Sexual differences Females larger than males.
Active period Nocturnal.
Enemies Jackal, hyaena, leopard, birds of prey.
Voice Quiet animals, soft grunt and scream loudly when handled.
Dentition I2/1 C0/0 P1/1 M3/3= 22

±3.5 cm

(Lepus capensis)

Cape hare

Setswana: Mutlwa	**Afrikaans:** Vlakhaas	**German:** Kaphaase
French: Le Lièvre sauteur	**Spanish:** Liebre saltarina	**Italian:** Lepre da Capo

Did you know?

Dentition of hares The skulls of larger rodents can be confused with those of hares, but the difference is that hares have a second pair of upper incisors. The first pair is large, sharp and rodent-like and the second pair is peg-like and situated directly behind the first. The cheek teeth are rootless and grow from an open root canal, being ever-growing, similar to those of the elephant.

Digestive system of hares Like other mammals, they do not produce the enzymes to digest cellulose and lignin but have

---

Order LAGOMORPHA
Family LEPORIDAE

Length m/f ± 50cm from nose to tail.
Weight m/f ±1,5-3.5kg.
Gestation ± 5-6 weeks.
Life span ±5 years.
Litter size One to three.
Habitat Open permanent water and sufficient food in the surrounding area.
Food Short grasses.
Water requirements Get enough water from food.
Social organization Solitary, mother and young.
Sexual differences Females are slightly larger than males.
Active period Nocturnal.
Enemies Small cats, jackals, birs of prey.
Voice They are quiet but can scream when caught or handled.
Dentition I2/1 C0/0 P1/1 M3/3= 22

---

micro-organisms in the digestive tract to do it for them. They have evolved a unique method of obtaining the maximum energy from their food source by the practice of coprophagy. This is when they re-ingest their own faeces to ensure complete diges-tion and to replenish the micro-bial fauna of the intestinal tract. They produce two types of faecal pellets, the one being the normal hard pellets which are produced during the day and are often seen on the ground. The second type is excreted at night and is soft, dark-coloured and gelat-inous. The hare re-ingests this directly from the anus. This pellet is formed in the caecum and it consists of countless bacteria. After re-ingestion, these pellets are not chewed and mixed with other food in the stomach, but lodged separately in the fundus of the stomach. The soft faeces are covered by a mem-brane and they continue to ferment in the stomach for many hours. One of the

fermentation products is lactic acid - a building block for protein. Studies have shown that the Cape hare practises coprophagy during the day and not at night like the scrub hare.

Voice They vocalise (scream) only when in distress.

Breeding The availability of food determines their rate of breeding. With a gestation of 42 days, they can breed up to four times per year but it is usually less often.

±3.5 cm

Rock hyrax
(Procavia capensis)

Setswana: Pela / Tshwanyê	**Afrikaans:** Klipdassie	**German:** Klippschliefer
French: Le daman de rocher	**Spanish:**	**Italian:** Marmotta

Did you know?

Closely related species A hyrax that often shares a habitat with the rock hyrax, is the yellow-spotted hyrax (*Heterohyrax brucei*). They often intermingle but never interbreed, despite their physical likeness. Both have light spots above the eye, but those of *H. brucei* are very prominent.

Dentition They have two incisors at the top and four at the bottom. The top incisors are enlarged and tusk-like. Like elephant tusks,

they grow throughout their life. They are mainly used as weapons but also for removing bark and to pull clumps of vegetation into their mouths. The rock hyrax (*Procavia*) is more of a grazer than a browser, and therefore has high-crowned cheek teeth (hypsodont) to accommodate wear. Their digestive system is also specialised to obtain sufficient nutrients from the dry, coarse grasses they feed on. The yellow-spotted hyrax (*Heterohyrax*) is more of a browser and has low-crowned teeth.

Male sexual organs The male sexual organs differ markedly in the two hyraxes, probably one of the reasons why they do not interbreed. The penis of *Heterohyrax* is up to 6cm long and is located under the belly. The rock hyrax has a smaller penis, located close to the anus. Incredibly, the testes of the rock hyrax increase ±20 times in size during the mating season!

Urine The white urine marks left on rocks consist of chrystallised calcium carbonate. Early colonists gathered the crystallised urine on the rocks and sold

it as a medicine under the name 'hyracium'. The urine itself has also been used medicinally for centuries by many African tribes. It was obtained by killing a hyrax and emptying the bladder. Hyrax urine is rich in nitrate of ammonia and was used as a sterilising liquid. It was specfically used for a leopard bite by the Zulu tribe in the past. Incidentally, all urine, even human urine, is sterile.

Order HYRACOIDEA
Family PROCAVIIDAE

Length m/f ±35-60cm.
Weight m ±3-5.5kg, f ±2-4kg.
Gestation ±7,5-8 months.
Life span ±12 years.
Litter size Up to six.
Habitat Rocky outcrops.
Food Mainly grass but also herbs and trees.
Water requirements They ususally get enough from food.
Social organization Gregarious, ±25 in group, territorial, one male, several female and offspring.
Sexual differences Males are larger than females.
Active period Diurnal.
Enemies Leopard, large birds of prey, caracal.
Voice Varied, a sharp alarm bark to a scream, growl and snort.
Dentition I1/2 C0/0 P4/3 M3/3 = 32

(Atelerix frontalis)

Hedgehog

Setswana: Tlhong / Setlhong	**Afrikaans:** Krimpvarkie
German: Igel	**French:** Herisson

Did you know?

Social structure Hedgehogs are solitary, except when the mother is raising her young.

Habitat They show a preference for habitats with sparse grass cover and are thus often found in overgrazed areas with dense herbivore populations.

Shelters The hedgehog travels through its home range and have various shelters, often just under thick layers of leaves or hollow tree trunks but they do also burrow to a limited extent.

Defence mechanism The hedgehog has a unique ability to curl up into a ball when alarmed, and its anatomy is specifically

Order INSECTIVORA
Family ERINACEIDAE

Length m/f ±16 - 24cm from nose to tail.
Weight m/f ±250 - 1 200kg.
Gestation ± 5 weeks.
Life span ±3 years.
Litter size One to ten.
Habitat Varied. Avoid deserts and forests. Vegetation cover important for hiding.
Food Insects, earthworms, millipedes, small vertebrates.
Water requirements Get enough water from food.
Social organization Solitary, mother and young.
Sexual differences None.
Active period Nocturnal.
Enemies Small cats, jackals, birs of prey.
Voice Snort, growl and high-pitched alarm call.

designed for this. They have blunt ridges and short spines on their vertebrae, which will not interfere with the severe curving of the spine when rolled up. They also have a wide pelvis, which provides protection for the vulnerable head. It literally buries its head inside the pelvis. Most amazing is the specialised muscle that is attached to the forehead. It is called a hemispherical muscle because it forms a half-dome, stretching across the back and sides where the spines occur. The spines are embedded into this muscle. When the muscle contracts, it becomes a spherical bag into which the head and the legs are withdrawn (Kingdon, 1997). It is a very effective defence against smaller carnivores, but is is no match for an eagle or a large cat

Feet Their feet are well padded and clawed. They do dig for food and sometimes to make a shelter.

Senses Their sight is poor but their hearing and smell is exceptional. They locate insect prey underground both by hearing and by smell.

Hibernation When food is plentiful, hedgehogs lay down a thick layer of fat underneath the skin. It makes the skin appear almost translucent. In late May to July, they become increasingly lethargic and rarely emerge from their hides. They may remain in a state of hibernation for about six weeks or longer. Even in captivity, they become torpid. 'Torpid' means that the metabolism becomes slow and there is a loss of co-ordination. This state seems to be regulated entirely by temperature. As soon as it warms up, they become active again.

Reproduction The females are seasonally poly-estrous, which means they can breed more than once in summer as their gestation is only ±5 weeks and the young are weaned at ±5 weeks old. The young are born blind and naked with the tips of the spines just showing. They can have up to 11 pups.

R O D E N T S

Order RODENTIA

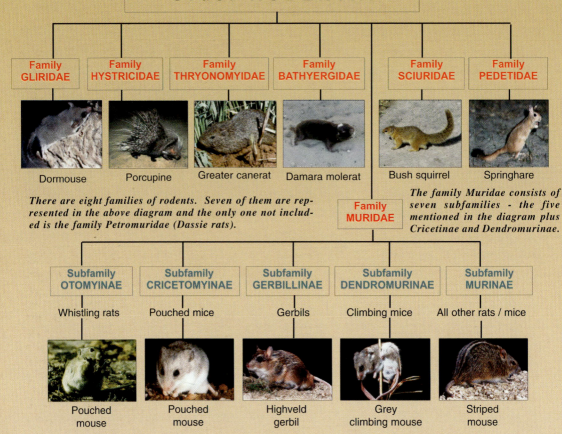

Family GLIRIDAE	Family HYSTRICIDAE	Family THRYONOMYIDAE	Family BATHYERGIDAE	Family SCIURIDAE	Family PEDETIDAE
Dormouse	Porcupine	Greater canerat	Damara molerat	Bush squirrel	Springhare

There are eight families of rodents. Seven of them are represented in the above diagram and the only one not included is the family Petromuridae (Dassie rats).

Family MURIDAE

The family Muridae consists of seven subfamilies - the five mentioned in the diagram plus Cricetinae and Dendromurinae.

Subfamily OTOMYINAE	Subfamily CRICETOMYINAE	Subfamily GERBILLINAE	Subfamily DENDROMURINAE	Subfamily MURINAE
Whistling rats	Pouched mice	Gerbils	Climbing mice	All other rats / mice
Pouched mouse	Pouched mouse	Highveld gerbil	Grey climbing mouse	Striped mouse

About rodents *Name:* The name 'rodent' is derived from the Latin '*rodere*', which means 'to gnaw'. Of all the mammalian orders, the *Rodentia* contains the most species. *Families and subfamilies:* The diagram above represents only the groups that are included in this book. There are eight families of rodents. Seven of them are represented in the above diagram and the only one not included is the family *Petromuridae* (Dassie rats). The biggest group, the family *Muridae* consists of seven subfamilies - the five mentioned in the above diagram plus *Cricetinae* and *Dendromurinae*. *Skull:* The most common feature shared by all rodents is their basic skull structure, specifically their dentition. Animals that do not need to open their mouths very wide, like hares and rodents that nibble, have a point of articulation of the jaw higher than the tooth row. The coronoid process of the mandible is absent. *Dentition:* They have prominent, ever-growing gnawing teeth in the front of the mouth. These consist of the lower and upper incisors and they occlude against each other in such a way as to keep them razor-sharp. There is a big space (diastema) between the incisors and the cheek teeth and they lack canines. They have ±20 teeth.

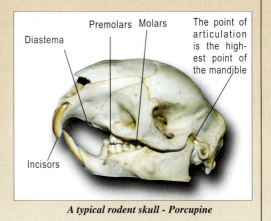

Diastema · Premolars Molars · The point of articulation is the highest point of the mandible · Incisors

A typical rodent skull - Porcupine

(*Cryptomys damarensis*) **Damara molerat**

Setswana: Serathi / Serunya	**Afrikaans:** Damarase vaalmol	**German:**
French:	**Spanish:**	**Italian:**

Molerat heap

Did you know?

Molerats versus golden moles

Molerats should not be confused with golden moles, which belong to the order *Insectivora*. Molerats eat bulbs and corms but moles are insect eaters. Their mole heaps look similar and they sometimes share the same tunnels. Read more about golden moles on pg 113.

Habitat and food

Very few mammals can compete with the outstanding evolutionary record of the molerat. As a member of the rodent family they have taken

> **Order** RODENTIA
> **Suborder** HYSTRICOGNATHI
> **Family** BATHYERGIDAE
> **Subfamily** BATHYERGINAE

Length m/f ±15-20cm, tail ±2cm.
Weight m/f ±100g.
Gestation ±78 days (±2,5months).
Life span Not known.
Litter size ±4-10 young.
Habitat Sandy soils, Kalahari, loose alluvial sand.
Food Rhizomes, tubers, bulbs.
Water requirements They get enough moisture from their food.
Social structure Eusocial society, only one breeding female.
Sexual differences None.
Active period Nocturnal.
Enemies Leopard, jackal, hyaena, caracal, honey badger, owl.
Voice Silent, can scream loudly when handled.
Dentition I1/1 C0/0 P1/1 M3/3= 20

a major evolutionary leap quite contrary to their fast-running, surface-foraging relatives. They have opted to spend their entire lives underground. They dig long tunnels where they can shelter and feed on roots, rhizomes, bulbs, corms and tubers. Food gathering is done by all colony members and it is seasonal (during and after the rains). The food is stored in a central store.

Social organisation

The most fascinating aspect of molerats is their social behaviour, which is the first of its kind to be recorded in mammals. Professor Jennifer Jarvis has categorised them as 'eusocial' mammals. This means that they have the same social organisation as bees, ants and termites, complete with a queen, workers and soldiers! She found that molerats form colonies of about 20-40 animals.

Reproduction

Only the queen breeds. She forces the other females, through vicious aggression, to suppress their reproductive ability to such an extent that they do not come into estrous at all. When the queen dies, the remaining females fight for dominance and the winner becomes the new queen. As soon as her dominance is

established, she starts increasing in size. About one to six young are born two to three times per year after a 2,5 month gestation. The isolation of the colonies makes inbreeding in-evitable and the queen molerat has no choice but to mate with her brothers and sons, possibly her own father. During inbreeding, recessive genes tend to combine, resulting in certain abnormalities. However, Dr. Barry Lovegrove (1993) points out that in fast-breeding animals with large litters, the abnormal animals die without having any negative effect on the colony. All members of the colony are genetically as much as 80% related! That is why each individual takes part in the gathering of food, defending the colony and raising the pups - to ensure the successful survival of their own genes. The pups beg for the fecal pellets of the adults, which they eat to acquire the necessary micro-organisms for digestion.

Porcupine

(*Hystrix africaeaustralis*)

back. This sheds some light onto the age-old question of 'how do porcupines mate?' However, it does not change the answer - 'very carefully!'. They give birth only once a year as gestation is ±3 months and lactation another ±3 months. The female does not cycle while lactating.

Young They are born with eyes open, incisor teeth fully erupted and short spines. Even though they become sexually mature at ±9-18 months, females will not conceive while still in the natal group (van Aarde, 1987). Both the male and the female offspring will disperse at full maturity to find mates of their own.

Did you know?

Social structure Porcupines are monogamous and one of the few animals to mate for life. They live in extended family groups consisting of a male and female and consecutive litters of their offspring.

Thermoregulation Porcupines have a wide tolerance for heat and cold. In summer they reduce their metabolic rate and in winter they reduce heat loss to adjust to the extremes (Haim, et.al, 1990).

Digestive system They are notorious for having a higher tolerance for plant poisons than most other animals. Their diet is varied and their digestive system can cope with almost everything. The stomach is muscular and the caecum is enlarged to ensure efficient digestion of fibrous plant material as well as protein (van Jaarsveld,1983).

Bones There are often bones around and in their den. They gnaw on them as a source of phosphates and calcium. It has been found that in captivity they develop osteophagia if they do not get these minerals (Duthie & Skinner, 1986).

Breeding van Aarde (1985) found that daily physical contact between male and female is required for normal cyclic ovarian activity. The female initiates mating by presenting her rear and lifting her tail. Surprisingly, they mate in the normal position with the front feet of the male on the female's

Order RODENTIA
Suborder HYSTRICOGNATHI
Family HYSTRIGIDAE

Height m/f ±84cm.
Weight m/f ±10-19kg, f ±10-24kg.
Gestation ±3 months.
Life span ±20 years.
Litter size ±1-3.
Habitat Woodland and scrub.
Food Roots, bulbs, rhizomes, vegetables, fruit, bones.
Water requirements They usually get enough water from their food but will also drink.
Social structure They mate for life and form loose groups of about 4.
Sexual differences Females heavier.
Active period Nocturnal.
Enemies Lion, leopard, hyaena.
Voice Growl, sniff and rattle their tail quills when alarmed.
Dentition I1/1 C0/0 P1/1 M3/3= 20

(*Thryonomys swinderianus*)   **Greater cane rat**

Setswana: Sepoopoo	**Afrikaans:** Groot rietrot	**German:** Grosse Rohrratt
French: L'Aulacode grand	**Spanish:** Rata de caña de azucar	**Italian:** Toio da canna da zucchero

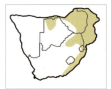

Did you know?

Name The genus name 'Thryonomys' is derived from the Greek 'thryon' = 'reed' and 'mys' = 'mouse'.

Anatomy These exceptionally large, rat-like creatures are surpassed only by the porcupine in size in the order *Rodentia*. Despite their large size, being about 50-80cm long and about 5-8kg in weight, they enjoy a very secretive existence and are seldom seen. They have relatively short tails (about 18cm) and the muzzle is extended, forming a fleshy pad that overhangs the nostrils. This is used mainly to demonstrate territorial aggres-

> **Order** RODENTIA
> **Suborder** HYSTRICOGNATHI
> **Family** THRYONOMYIDAE

Length m/f body ±50cm, tail ±20cm.
Weight m/f ±5-8kg.
Gestation ±5 months (very long for a rodent).
Life span ±4 years.
Litter size ±4-8.
Habitat Reedbeds.
Food Roots and shoots of reeds and grasses.
Water requirements Water dependent.
Social structure Solitary or groups of 8-10.
Sexual differences Males are larger than females.
Active period Mainly night.
Enemies Leopard, jackal, hyaena, eagle, pythons, people.
Voice Deep warning growl, grunt when feeding.
Dentition I1/1 C0/0 P1/1 M3/3= 20

sion when they butt each other head-on. Their bristly hairs readily fall out when handled by humans - an adaptation to escape predation.

Habitat preference They have very specific habitat requirements, and reeds (*Phragmites australis*) or grasses with thick, reed-like stems and permanent water are essential. This explains their absence in the drier southwestern corner of South Africa. They form a distinct network of tunnels or runs among the reeds or in stands of Cottonwool grass (*Imperata cylindrica*), where they move around in relative safety. Canerats are excellent swimmers and usually seek refuge in the water when threatened. They are nocturnal and lie up on flattened reedbeds during the day.

Reproduction The Greater canerat has a very long gestation period for its size - five months, which is longer than that of a lion (3,5 months). The long gestation is a survival mechanism to supply sufficient time for the

development of the ±4 young which are born precocially. This means that they have hair, their eyes are open and they can follow the mother around within the first hour of their lives.

Predators Pythons, leopards and baboons prey on these animals but man is by far their greatest enemy. It has been reported that 177 tons of canerat meat is purchased annually in the city of Accra, Ghana, to supply the restaurants where it is served as a delicacy. They are hunted by means of dogs that chase them along the runs into fall-traps.

Cape ground squirrel　*(Xerus inauris)*

Setswana: Sekata-mosima / Semane	**Afr:** Waaierstertgrondeekhoring	**German:** Kap-erdhornchen
French: Écureuil foisseur	**Spanish:** Ardila terrestre	**Italian:** Scoiattolo

Did you know?

Habitat They live in warrens on the ground in arid semi-desert. In Botswana they occur in the Kalahari and prefer open areas, especially in calcareous soils near pans where the harder soil is ideal for excavating warrens.

Social structures They live in colonies of 20-35 and they are active by day. The social unit consists of several females and their young. Males only join the group when a female is in estrous. There is one dominant female that defends the territory more vigorously than the others.

±3 cm

Bachelor males establish territories but are much more mobile than the females.

Digging Ground squirrels are well equipped to dig and use their sharp incisor teeth to cut roots.

Warrens The warrens consists of a complicated network of tunnels. They are about 1m deep but are occasionally deeper. Temperatures in the warrens are very mild compared to the extremes of the Kalahari. Winter temperatures are ±13° and summer temperatures 28°C. There are chambers for nesting, which are lined with grass. They sometimes share a warren with the Yellow mongoose and/or the Suricate. It is interesting to note that they usually live in harmony, but the Yellow mongoose will occasionally kill and eat injured or sick ground squirrels.

Thermoregulation Ground squirrels make use of their burrows to regulate their body temperature. They also sand-bathe on their tummies to get cool. The bushy tail acts

as a built-in umbrella, which they use to create shade.

Reproduction They have their young throughout the year and they breed only once a year. The litter consist of one to three pups that weigh ±20g at birth. The pups are altricial (born blind and naked) and they only leave the burrows at ±40 days old.

Order RODENTIA
Suborder SCIUROGNATHI
Family SCIURIDAE

Length ±25cm, tail ±18cm.
Weight ±500 - 1 100g.
Gestation ± 6-7 weeks, not quite sure.
Life span ±8 years.
Litter size One to three.
Habitat Near pans or higher, ground in sandy-loam soil.
Food Rhizomes, tubers, grass stems, fruit, insects, leaves.
Water requirements Not dependent on surface water.
Social structure Colonies of 20-35 of females and young.
Sexual differences None.
Active period Nocturnal.
Enemies Leopard, jackal, caracal, birds of prey, snakes.
Voice Silent, can scream loudly when handled.
Dentition I1/1 C0/0 P1/1 M3/3 = 20

(Paraxerus cepapi) # Tree Squirrel

Setswana: Setlhorê	**Afrikaans:** Boomeekhoring	**German:** Buschörnchen
French: L'Ecureuil des bois	**Spanish:** Ardilla de arbol	**Italian:** Scoiattolo da Iberto

Did you know?

Habitat preference Tree squirrels are more closely associated with *Acacia* and mopane woodland than with any other vegetation type because of the natural holes in these trees that the squirrels use for nesting.

Social structure They usually form small groups consisting of variable groupings. I observed three males that shared a nest for a few months or it may be a female with young or a male, female and young. They are territorial and the territories are defended by the males. They recognise each other by smell. They mark each other by dragging their anal glands over the back of a group member.

Jumping They have the ability to leap up to 2m from tree to tree. Their strong hind legs are suitable for this. Their ankle bones are adapted so that the feet point backward when they hang from their feet.

Food Although they are mainly vegetarian, eating fruits, flowers, seeds and shoots, they also eat termites, aphids and ants at certain times of the year. They bury hard foods such as seeds and it is quite comical to watch them as they take all precautions to do it 'under cover' so that another squirrel will not locate their cache. They do not bury their food all in the same place as some other squirrel species do.

Reproduction When a female comes into estrous, she advertises the fact by a more excited version of the normal alarm call, which may continue for hours. Several males will be attracted, also from other groups. Viljoen (1977) found that the vocalisation of the female seems to stimulate estrous in other nearby females, resulting in synchronisation. The births can take place at any time of the year, but are more common in summer.

Order RODENTIA
Suborder SCIUROGNATHI
Family SCIURIDAE

Length Body ±15cm, tail ±14cm.
Weight m ±100-240g,
f ±120 -260g.
Gestation ±8 weeks.
Life span ±8 years.
Litter size One to three.
Habitat Mainly Acacia thornveld and mopane woodland.
Food Leaves, flowers, seeds, fruit, bark, berries.
Water requirements They get enough from food, will also drink.
Social structure Varied groups, female and young with or without 1-2 males. Territorial.
Sexual differences Females slightly larger.
Active period Diurnal.
Enemies Genets, birds of prey, snakes, leopard, caracal.
Voice Bird-like "chook-chook-chook" sound or 'chic-chirrrrrrr'.
Dentition I1/1 C0/0 P1/1 M3/3= 20

± 2,5 cm

Springhare

(*Pedetes capensis*)

Setswana: Ntlolê	**Afrikaans:** Springhaas	**German:** Springhase
French: Liévre sauteur	**Spanish:** Liebre saltarina	**Italian:** Lepre salante

Did you know?

Habitat Springhares prefer short grass areas in sandy soil, often near pans. Their burrows are mostly in raised grass fringes around pans, where they are safe from flooding during the rainy season. They do not favour areas with tall grass.

Burrows They dig extensive burrows which can be up to 45m long and have as many as 11 entrances. One tunnel system is usually only occupied by a single springhare and there are no chambers or bedding material present. They often close the opening from the inside.

Food Springhares feed almost exclusively on grass but they are highly selective in their preference for certain plant parts, wastefully discarding the rest. The front feet are used to manipulate the food. In the Kruger Park, Couch grass (*Cynodon dactylon*), is probably the most heavily utilised by springhares, but only the leaves and especially the rhizomes are eaten.

Burrowing and hopping The springhare is perfectly adapted for burrowing by digging with the front claws and clearing away the sand with the hind legs. Their front feet are equipped with long nails for digging. The long hind legs enable them to move very fast in typical 'kangaroo-style'. This style of movement makes it a 'saltator', as opposed to a 'cursor', which run on all four legs.

Impact on pastures

Because of their extensive burrows and their wasteful feeding habit, they can have a negative impact on natural pastures. However, their distribution is patchy and their foraging very localised, diminishing the overall impact. In fact, their extensive burrows have a valuable function in aerating the soil.

Order RODENTIA
Suborder SCIUROGNATHI
Family PEDETIDAE

Length Body ±40cm, tail ±40cm.
Weight ±2,5-3,8kg.
Gestation ± 10½ weeks.
Life span ±7 years.
Litter size One.
Habitat Near pans or higher, ground in sandy-loam soil.
Food Rhizomes, tubers, grass.
Water requirements They get enough water from their food.
Social structure Mainly solitary or mother with young.
Sexual differences None.
Active period Nocturnal.
Enemies Leopard, jackal, hyaena, lion, caracal, man.
Voice Silent, can scream loudly when handled.
Dentition I1/1 C0/0 P1/1 M3/3= 20

±4cm

±5cm

S M A L L   R O D E N T S

Family Gliridae

Woodland doormouse (Graphiurus murinus)

Habitat: They prefer dense woodland since they live almost entirely in trees (arboreal). They often choose an area near a beehive. *Food:* Dead bees, honey, wax, bagworms, termites, millipedes, nestlings, seeds, fruit. *Active:* Nocturnal. *Regeneration of tail:* They have the partial ability to regenerate their tail. In African species an exaggerated brush of hair will grow but in European forms the regeneration of the caudal (tail) vertebrae has actually been documented.

Woodland doormouse (Graphiurus murinus)

Family Muridae   Subfamily Murinae

Water rat (Dasymys incomtus)

Habitat: As the name implies, they occur in swamps, reedbeds and riverine vegetation and are in fact partially aquatic, being able to swim well. They have tunnels among rotting vegetation, which provides them with relative safety. *Food:* Mostly vegetarian, shoots of water plants, grass seeds, also insects. *Nests:* Very elaborate nests consisting of a 'ball' of vegetation, ±20cm in diameter. They typically consist of two nests, a superficial one at the top and the real nest below. From there a tunnel leads into the water (±30cm deep), of which the blind end is completely submerged, suggesting that the water rat will swim the last bit to escape into the water.

Water rat (Dasymys incomtus)

Pencil-tailed tree rat (Thallomys paedulcus)

Habitat: They are arboreal (live in trees), preferring *Acacia* trees but also living in Jackalberry trees and others. *Food:* Mainly *Acacia* seeds, pods, leaves and gum of Acacia trees, as well as insects. They sometimes create their own source of food by making grooves in the bark of Acacia trees, which then exude gum as the tree tries to repair itself. The Tree rats return nightly to lick up the gum (Tim Liversedge, pers. com.). The photograph on the right illustrates this. *Nests:* They build large untidy nests high up and towards the outer branches of *Acacia* trees or in hollow tree trunks. The nesting material often overflow and consists of grass, leaves and fine twigs. In the Kalahari these nests can aggravate veld fires and often lead to the destruction of the tree. They have regular branch 'highways', which are marked by perineal glands. *Active:* Nocturnal.

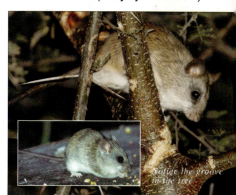
Notice the groove in the tree

Pencil-tailed tree rat
(Thallomys paedulcus)

Red veld rat (Aethomys chrysophilus)

Name: 'Aethomys' is from the Greek 'aithos' = 'sunburnt', probably in reference to this rat's colour. Interestingly, the name 'Ethiopia' is from the same root. *Habitat:* It occurs mostly in open woodland or open scrub in alluvial and sandy soils, and often on the fringes of pans. *Food:* Grass seeds, kernels, other vegetation. *Active:* Nocturnal. *Habits:* They are less shy than other species. *Nests:* They prefer to make nests above ground but will also burrow.

Red veld rat (Aethomys chrysophilus)

Namaqua rock mouse (Aethomys namaquensis)

Habitat: They have a wide habitat tolerance ranging from rocky outcrops, riverine woodland and open scrub to fringes of pans. **Food:** Omnivorous, it favours Camelthorn seeds. **Active:** Nocturnal. **Nests:** They are communal and build large domed nests of sticks and grass. Nests can be as large as 1,2m wide x 90cm high. Underneath are subterranean tunnels for escape.

Namaqua rock mouse
(Aethomys namaquensis)

Four-striped mouse (Rhabdomys pumilio)

Name: From 'rhobdo', meaning 'rod', referring to the markings on the back. **Habitat:** Varied, preferring grassland and vlei country. They avoid areas with low or no grass cover like the Karoo. **Food:** Grass seeds, also *Acacia* seeds and occasionally eggs, nestlings, snails and bark. By damaging the bark of young seedlings, they can cause tremendous damage to forest plantations, where they occur in large enough populations. **Nests:** They burrow into the ground at a slanting angle, up to 50cm below the surface. **Indicator species:** They do not favour disturbed areas and can be described as a 'grassland specialists'. They are thus an indicator species, indicating stable conditions in grassland and representing the late stages in succession. The Multimammate mouse (*Praomys natalensis*), on the other hand, occurs mainly in unstable areas (see pg 78).

Four-striped mouse (Rhabdomys pumilio)

Single-striped mouse (Lemniscomys griselda)

Name: 'Lemnisco' means 'banded', referring to the dorsal stripe on its back. **Habitat:** Grassland, shrubland and *Acacia* veld, also *Terminalia* sandveld. **Food:** Mostly grass seeds and other vegetation matter. **Active:** Mostly diurnal. **Nests:** They do burrow but normally dwell on the surface, breeding in above-ground grass nests.

Single-striped mouse
(Lemniscomys griselda)

Pygmy mouse (Mus minutoides)

Size: The Pygmy mouse is one of the smallest mammals in the world, being only ±10cm long, including the tail. The body and head is only ±5,5cm. **Habitat:** It occurs in most vegetation types and can tolerate rainfall from ±200mm to below 700mm per annum. They often occur on the edges of pans and in riverine woodland. **Food:** They are omnivorous (grains, seeds, fruits, insects). **Population explosion:** Their numbers rise and fall with those of the Multimammate mouse (*Praomys natalensis*), probably because the larger species becomes a predator shield. Because of their small size, they are not severely influenced by the depleted resources as they manage to benefit from the wasteful feeding of the larger rodents.

Pygmy mouse (Mus minutoides)

Spiny mouse (Acomys spinosissimus)

Name: 'Acomys' means 'a sharp point' and 'spinosus' means 'like a spine' referring to its spiny coat. **Habitat:** Prefers dry woodland and rocky places, also mopane woodland. **Food:** Mainly beetles, ants, termites, millipedes, spiders, snails, also seeds. **Nests:** Among rock crannies or tree roots. **Active:** Predominantly nocturnal.

Spiny mouse (Acomys spinosissimus)

Multimammate mouse
(Proaomys [Mastoys] natalensis)

Anatomy: The female has a record 12 mammae on each side of the body, hence the common name 'Multimammate mouse'. Gravid females have been recorded with 24 fetuses (Smithers, 1975). **Habitat:** They have a very wide habitat tolerance, showing a preference for disturbed areas. **Food:** Seeds of annual grasses, exotics and *Acacia* trees. They mainly eat grains but also insects. **Habits:** They are nocturnal, communal and terrestrial. **Indicator species:** They are one of the first species to invade areas after habitat destruction has taken place, such as fire or man-made disturbance. They thrive on annuals, weeds and exotics. They are mostly associated with the secondary phase of succession. As plant succession proceeds to more stable conditions, *Praomys* will be replaced by grassland specialists such as the Striped mouse (*Rhabdomys pumilio*) and in

Multimammate mouse (Praomys natalensis)

swampy areas eventually by the Vlei rat (*Otomys* spp.). **Population explosions:** When a good rainy season follows a long drought it my lead to population explosions, especially in animals with a short gestation period such as rodents. Within two years the population will usually fall to below normal as they have the tendency to breed at an above-normal rate and then proceed to deplete their own resources. Inbreeding and intense intra-specific contact will soon lead to abnormalities and disease. Abnormalities such as sores on the feet and eyes and abnormal sexual organs have been observed during such population explosions. **Association with man:** They are very closely associated with man. Because of their population increase during good years, they can be very serious crop pests and carriers of disease. **Disease:** They are intermediate hosts for Bubonic Plague and Lassa Fever.

Family Muridae   Subfamily Otomyinae

Brant's whistling rat (Parotomys brantsii)

Name: They are called 'Whistling rats' because of the sharp, high-pitched whistle that they utter when alarmed. **Habitat:** They occur in the dry southwestern parts of Botswana and are common in the Kgalagadi Transfrontier Park. They burrow in hard, sandy soils between dunes (dune troughs) and are often associated with the Driedoring, *Rhigozum trichotomum* (de Graaff, 1981). **Warrens:** They live in a warren system that covers ±4x6m, which has up to 20 entrances. The tunnels are ±8cm in diameter. **Nests:** Inside the tunnel system is a nest chamber of ±30cm high, consisting of finely shredded plant material. **Food:** They feed exclusively on plants such as grasses, sedges and small legumes. They carry the food to the nest and discard the unpalatable pieces at the nest entrance. They sit on their haunches when feeding. **Activity:** Brant's whistling rats are active during the day and can often be sen in the Kalahari. They are most active early in the morning.

Brant's whistling rat (Parotomys brantsii)

Pouched mouse (*Saccostomus campestris*)

Pouched mouse (*Saccostomus campestris*)

Name: From 'sacco' = 'sac' and 'stomus' = mouth', referring to its cheek pouches. **Habitat:** They have a wide tolerance for various habitats from open veld to forests. **Food:** Seeds of various woody species. It is a true hoarder and food is transported in the cheek pouches. **Active:** Nocturnal. **Social structure:** They are terrestrial, solitary or occur in pairs. They have very sluggish movements compared to other rodents, making it easier to photograph them. **Nests:** They burrow and seal the entrance during the day. **Pouch:** It can hold a mopane fruit (±3,5cm in diameter) or up to 60 sunflower seeds in the pouch. They take the food back to the nest where they can eat it in safety. Leftovers can often be seen infront of the nests. **Social structure:** They are solitary. **Breeding:** Gestation is ±21 days. The mother occasionally carries the young in her cheek pouch when moving them.

Notice the full cheek pouches

Notice the full pouches

Bushveld gerbil (*Tatera leucogaster*)

Bushveld gerbil (*Tatera leucogaster*)

Name: From '*leucogaster*', meaning 'white belly'. **Habitat:** Open woodland in sandy soils, also sandy alluvium. They do not occur in areas with less than 250mm of rainfall per year. **Food:** Seeds of trees, grasses, rhizomes. They do not hoard food but they do sometimes cover the food with soil. **Habits:** They are communal. **Nests:** Warrens are relatively small and scattered, usually at the bases of trees. Ramps of loose soil is an indication that the warren is active, as the gerbils clean out the nest every night. **Disease:** It is a reservoir of the Bubonic Plague virus (*Yersinia pestis*).

Gerbil nests in the Kalahari

Highveld gerbil (*Tatera brantsii*)

Habitat: They occur in peaty soils around marshes, also in molerat tunnels, making their own entrances into these. They also occur in sandy soil and can tolerate arid conditions with rainfall less than 250mm per year. They are common in the Kgalagadi Transfrontier Park. **Food:** They eat bulbs of grasses, seeds, insects. They do not hoard. **Nests:** They make elaborate warrens in sandy ground. Fresh earth at the entrances show that the nest is active. The nests can be huge and in the Kalahari they often cause vehicles to get stuck if they make their warrens in the middle of sandy road tracks. **Disease:** They are parasitised by fleas which breed in the burrows. The fleas act as intermediate hosts for the Bubonic Plague virus (*Yersinia pestis*), and are one of the main sources thereof.

Highveld gerbil (*Tatera branrsii*)

Star-tailed gerbil
(*Desmodillus auricularis*)

Name: From '*desmo*' = 'similar' and '*illus*' = '*gerbillus*', in other words similar to the gerbils. **Distribution:** It is not common in the Kruger Park but it has been collected along the Limpopo river, just west of the park. **Habitat:** In and around dry pans. **Food:** Seeds of the Devil's thorn (*Tribulus terrestris*) as well as other seeds and insects. **Nests:** They burrow up to 2m deep. They are true larder-hoarders. **Active:** Nocturnal.

Star-tailed gerbil
(*Desmodillus auricularis*)

Hairy-footed gerbil (*Gerbillurus paeba*)

Distribution: It has not been collected in the Kruger Park, but it does occur in the bushveld west of Punda Maria. It is very common in the arid areas of Botswana, Namibia and the western Cape. **Habitat:** They occur in desert and sub-desert regions and prefer sandy alluvium and sandy soils in light woodland. **Food:** Seeds of grasses and trees. **Habits:** Terrestrial, nocturnal. **Nests:** Their burrows are similar but much smaller than those of *Tatera* (Bushveld and Highveld gerbils, pg 79). **Disease:** They host the tick *Rhiicephalus capensis* that hosts a protozoan, *Theileria parva*. This causes East Coast fever in cattle.

Hairy-footed gerbil
(*Gerbillurus paeba*)

Family Muridae   Subfamily Dendromurinae

Grey pygmy climbing mouse
(*Dendromus melanotis*)

Habitat: They favour swamp fringes with tall grasses such as *Hyparrhenia* and *Hyperthelia*. They will also nest under carpets of Salvinia in the Okavango Delta. **Food:** Seeds and insects, even small snakes, lizards and birds. They climb onto grass stalks to get to the seeds. **Habits:** Terrestrial and nocturnal but not gregarious. They are either solitary or a pair will share a hole. They are extremely aggressive and, in captivity, have been known to fight to death with an intruder. **Nests:** They burrow ±50cm deep.

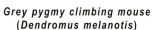

Grey pygmy climbing mouse
(*Dendromus melanotis*)

Chestnut climbing mouse
(*Dendromus mystacalis*)

Habitat: They occur in grassland and favour floodplain grassland and low-lying areas. In Botswana they occur only in the Kasane area. They favour thatching grasses such as *Hyparrhenia* and *Hyperthelia* spp. **Food:** They are graminivorous (eat grains) but will also eat insects. **Nests:** Exposed places high up in shrubby vegetation. **Habits:** They are very aggressive.

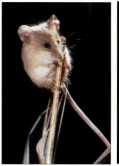

Chestnut climbing mouse
(*Dendromus mystacalis*)

Order INSECTIVORA

The order *Insectivora* is often described as the 'scrap-basket' order for primitive, small mammals that feed on insects. The four groups in the order are the tenrecs (not in South Africa), golden moles, shrews and hedgehogs. The elephant shrews were formerly in this order but are now placed in their own order - *Macroscelidae*. For the purpose of this book, only the musk shrews and the golden mole will be included. They all have a long, mobile nose and a cylindrical, stout skull. Both the latter features are used to bulldoze insects out of their retreats. They are a very ancient group with their ancestry dating back more than 40 million years. Their incisors act as pincers and their molars and premolars as shredders for the tough insect chitin. They are highly territorial and have scent glands on their flanks, hence the name 'musk-shrews'. Their metabolism remains active throughout the day and night, at a very high rate with bursts of increased activity. They will die if they are deprived of water or food for even a short time. In captivity, it was found that they eat between one third to two thirds of their body weight in one day (Meester, 1963). Their lifespan in the wild is estimated at only 16 months and in captivity they live for ±2,5 years (Skinner & Smithers, 1990). They will attack large insects similar to their own size, such as large grasshoppers.

Family Soricidae   Subfamily Crocidurinae

Lesser red musk shrew (Crocidura hirta)

Lesser red musk shrew (*Crocidura hirta*)

Habitat: They are very adaptable, preferring low bushes for cover. They occur in the Okavango and Kalahari and are not dependent on water. **Habits:** Active throughout the 24 hours in a day to maintain their fast metabolism. Usually solitary or in family groups. **Food:** Mainly insects. **Breeding:** Gestation is only 18 days and there are usually ±5 pups.

Reddish-grey musk shrew (Crocidura cyanea)

Reddish-grey musk shrew (*Crocidura cyanea*)

Habitat: Very adaptable, varying from the south-west arid zone to montane forest to grassland, but seems to be absent in the central parts of Southern Africa. **Activity:** Night and day, feeding about every hour. **Food:** Insects. **Breeding:** The pups are born hairless.

Swamp musk shrew (Crocidura mariquensis)

Swamp musk shrew (*Crocidura mariquensis*)

Habitat: It prefers a moist habitat such as reedbeds, and thick semi-aquatic grassland along rivers. It is often associated with Vlei rats (*Otomys* spp.). **Food:** Insects. **Nests:** In clumps of tussock grasses on slightly raised ground.

Family Chrysochloridae

Golden mole (*Amblysomus cf. hottentotus*)

Distribution: No golden moles have been recorded in Botswana, but they do occur in surrounding areas. **Anatomy:** They should not be confused with molerats, which are rodents and have protruding incisor teeth. Golden moles have a horny pad on the point of the muzzle, which encloses the nostrils. They have 36-40 teeth, compared to 20 in the molerat. **Size:** They vary from ±8-12cm. **Claws:** They have long, pointed claws that are hollow underneath, almost knife-like, to cut through the earth. Their back feet have webs to push the soil back as they burrow. **Habitat:** They prefer light soils such as sandy loam. They often co-exist with the Common molerat, sometimes even sharing a burrow with them. **Food:** They feed on insects and earthworms. They are very sensitive to movement on the soil, like the fluttering of a moth, and will emerge swiftly to capture it. **Activity:** They are mainly nocturnal, at which time they may move on the surface.

Golden mole
(Amblysomus cf. hottentotus)

Order MACROSCELIDAE

This is an archaic order and it shared a common ancestry with hares some 100 million years ago. All members in this group are commonly known as elephant shrews. They are insect feeders and were formerly placed in the order *Insectivora*. Their most diagnostic feature is their elongated snout or 'trunk', earning them their common name of 'elephant shrew'. Another unique feature is their 40-42 teeth, about twice as many as the normal 20 teeth for rodents. The normal dental formula is i3/3 C1/1 P4/4 M2/2=40. Some species have an extra premolar. They have large eyes and hunt mainly small insects such as ants. They have extremely long tongues that can curl over the 'trunk' to clean themselves after eating. Their hind legs are longer than their front legs but they mostly run instead of hop. They are active day and night with a very high metabolic rate. Like the *Insectivora*, their lifespan is also short, ±2-3 years (Skinner & Smithers, 1990).

Family Macroscelididae   Subfamily Macroscelidinae

Rock elephant shrew
(*Elephantulus myurus*)

Habitat: They are confined to rocky outcrops and nest in rock crannies, preferring vegetation cover to hide their nests. They live close to the Short-snouted elephant shrew (*E. brachyrhynchus*), but the latter occurs on the flat, sandy areas surrounding the rocky outcrops that *E. myurus* inhabits. **Activity:** Diurnal. **Food:** Small insects, termites and ants. They often forage in dassie middens. **Voice:** When they squeak in alarm, they open the mouth and the trunk is curled upwards. They make a purring noise by stamping their feet.

Rock elephant shrew
(*Elephantulus myurus*)

Bushveld elephant shrew
(*Elephantulus intufi*)

Habitat: They occur in the arid southwestern zone and are common in the Kalahari. In the central Kalahari, they are the only species of elephant shrew. Vegetation cover is very important to them. They are absent in the Kruger Park but do occur along the Limpopo river. **Habits:** They are exclusively diurnal. They burrow under vegetation cover. They make a purring noise by stamping their feet in alarm. **Food:** Small insects. **Breeding:** They have 1-3 young that are born precocially (well-developed).

Bushveld elephant shrew
(*Elephantulus intufi*)

Short-snouted elephant shrew
(*Elephantulus brachyrhynchus*)

Habitat: They prefer well-watered areas and are common in the Okavango Delta. They prefer areas with dense grass cover, scrub and scattered trees. **Habits:** They are active during the day and night and are mostly solitary. **Food:** Insects, also seeds. **Breeding:** Only two or often only one young are born precocially. They soon feed independently. **Longevity:** All elephant shrews have a very short life span (±1,5 - 2,5 years).

Short-snouted elephant shrew
(*Elephantulus brachyrhynchus*)

B A T S

Order CHIROPTERA

Suborder MEGACHIROPTERA

Family PTEROPODIDAE

Fruit bats

Peter's epauletted fruit bat

Suborder MICROCHIROPTERA

Family MULOSSIDAE

Free-tailed bats

Little free-tailed bat

Family VESPERTILIONIDAE

Plain-faced bats

Yellow housebat

Family RHINOLOPHIDAE

Horseshoe bats

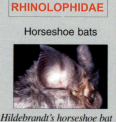

Hildebrandt's horseshoe bat

Family HIPPOSEDERIDAE

Leafnosed bats

Sundevall's leafnosed bat

Family NYCTERIDAE

Slit-fced bats

Common slit-faced bat

Interesting facts about bats

Location of prey *Megachiroptera* (fruit bats) do not make use of echolocation because they do not need to hunt. The familiar clicking sound made by them has more of a sexual significance as it is emitted only by the males. The *Microchiroptera* (insect feeders) have varying degrees of echolocation ability. They can all hunt in total darkness. Those with elaborate facial 'leafs' on their faces (like the horseshoe bats, the leafnosed bats and even the slit-faced bats), have the ability to hunt in thick vegetation. The plain-faced and free-tailed bats are mostly high, fast fliers. The bats both transmit and receive the sound impulses made by the larynx. A human can hear from ±20 vibrations per second to ±18 000. We cannot hear the sounds that bats emit because they go up to 230 000 vibrations per second. This number (230 000) represents the pitch. The other amazing thing is the frequency at which they emit the calls. It varies from a normal 100 calls per second, increasing up to about 1 000 calls per second when nearing the prey. They use low-frequency calls to detect prey of up to 10m away because low frequencies carry further in air. Just think of elephants that can emit low-frequency calls of less than 12 vibrations per second, enabling them to communicate over very long distances. High-frequency calls dissipate easier in air and are thus only used for locating prey up to ±6m away. Bats use different kinds of sound to get different information. A steady emission will allow them to detect direction and speed. This is based on the same principle of a car horn that falls in pitch as it passes, called the 'Doppler effect'.

Delayed reproduction Some of the plain-faced bats and the leaf-nosed bats employ various manners of delay during reproduction, varying from delayed implantation (*Miniopterus schreibersii*, pg 85 and *Scotophilus viridus*, pg 86), storage of sperm (*Nycticeinops schlieffeni*, pg 87) or retarded embryonic *growth* (*Hipposideros caffer*, pg 88).

FRUIT BATS
Order CHIROPTERA Suborder MEGACHIROPTERA Family PTEROPODIDAE

These are larger than other bats and have typical elongated, dog-like faces. They lack all the appendages and large ears of insect-eating bats because they do not employ echolocation to detect their food. They eat only fruit and locate it mainly by sight and smell.

Peter's epauletted fruit bat
(Epomophorus gambianus)

Habitat: This species occurs mainly in riverine woodland and ever-green forests that contain fruit-bearing trees. They very seldom occur in arid associations like *Acacia* or mopane, unless it is near riverine woodland. Their day roost is always in evergreen indigenous trees. They seem to favour fig trees such as the Sycamore fig (*Ficus sycomorus*). **Food:** Soft fruits such as wild figs and the berries of the Birdplum (*Berchemia discolor*). **Habits:** They are gregarious, forming groups of 10 to more than 100. They hang by their feet and are more

or less equally spaced. They forage alone. **Voice:** Their call is a continuous metallic 'ting-ting-ting' that is uttered by the male. It is one of the most common sounds of the African night. **Reproduction:** They have a single young. At first the baby clings to the nipple and is carried with the mother while foraging. Later she leaves it hanging. The mother and baby can often be seen hanging together until the baby is almost the same size as the mother.

Mother with baby

Peter's epauletted fruit bat
(*Epomophorus gambianus*)

FREE-TAILED BATS
Order CHIROPTERA Suborder MICROCHIROPTERA Family MULOSSIDAE

These are easy to recognise as a group with their free, mouse-like tails and wrinkled, bulldog faces. 'Mulossidae' means 'wrinkled face'. They are fast fliers and fly at least 20m from the ground.

Angola free-tailed bat
(Tadarida condylura)

Description: It is ±14cm long including the 4cm long tail. **Name:** The family name 'Mulossidae' refers to its likeness to a bulldog, with lots of wrinkles. **Habitat:** It occurs mainly in savanna woodland and riverine woodland. It does not occur in the arid southwestern zone of southern Africa and is therefore absent in the Kalahari. **Food:** They have powerful jaws, enabling them to feed on beetles and other tough insects. They are aerial feeders. They often roost with the Little free-tailed bat (*Tadarida pumila*) and they are both common house pests. **Habits:** They are gregarious,

Angola free-tailed bat
(*Tadarida condylura*)

usually occurring in larger groups. They often live in tree cracks but require a free drop to take to flight. **Reproduction:** They breed in summer and more than one pregnancy may occur in the breeding season. Gestation is ±85 days (±3 months) and a single young is born.

Little free-tailed bat
(Tadarida [Chaerephon] pumila)

Order CHIROPTERA   Suborder MICROCHIROPTERA   Family

Description: Its total length is ±9cm. It is the smallest of the free-tailed bats. **Habitat:** It occurs in savanna woodland, also in dry mopane veld. **Habits:** It is gregarious, forming colonies of more than 100 and in exceptional cases up to 2 500. They have a very fast flight. **Food:** They feed on insects, bugs, beetles, moths, *Hymenoptera*. They are fast, high-flying aerial feeders. **Reproduction:** Gestation is ±60 days (±2 months) and a single young is born. There may be more than one pregnancy in one breeding season.

Little free-tailed bat
(*Tadarida (Chaerephon) pumila*)

PLAIN-FACED BATS
Order CHIROPTERA   Suborder MICROCHIROPTERA   Family VESPERTILIONIDAE

The plain-faced bats comprise the largest group of the *Microchiroptera*. As the name implies, they lack the wrinkles and other leaf-like facial appendages of many other bats, suggesting that they do not need the advanced echolocation skills to catch their prey. They are better adapted to fly high and fast. In this group the second phalanx of the third digit is elongated, giving the wings a narrow, pointed shape, almost like those of swallows. This is an adaptation for fast flight and for migration. When folded, the wings have a bent appearance. These bats have characteristically small ears and highly raised foreheads. They cling with their toes and wing-claws to substrates and to other bats. They are therefore often referred to as 'clinging bats'. Some species in the family *Vespertilionidae* employ an interesting phenomenon called 'reproductive delay'. This can vary from delayed implantation (*Miniopterus schreibersii* and *Scotophilus viridus*), storage of sperm (*Nycticeinops schlieffeni*) or retarded embryonic growth (*Hipposideros caffer*).

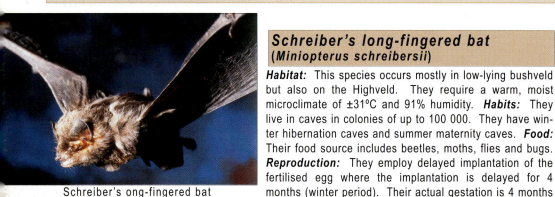

Schreiber's ong-fingered bat

Schreiber's long-fingered bat
(Miniopterus schreibersii)

Habitat: This species occurs mostly in low-lying bushveld but also on the Highveld. They require a warm, moist microclimate of ±31°C and 91% humidity. **Habits:** They live in caves in colonies of up to 100 000. They have winter hibernation caves and summer maternity caves. **Food:** Their food source includes beetles, moths, flies and bugs. **Reproduction:** They employ delayed implantation of the fertilised egg where the implantation is delayed for 4 months (winter period). Their actual gestation is 4 months but with the delay their gestation is effectively 8 months long. Considering their small size, 4 months is still a very long gestation. The young are usually born in December.

Cape serotine bat (Eptesicus capensis)

Habitat: It is very widespread south of the Sahara and occurs in savanna woodland. **Habits:** It occurs in small groups of 2-3. **Food:** They feed mainly on beetles and moths that occur in the canopy area of the woodland. When they leave their hide to forage, their flight is sluggish at first, at which time they are vulnerable to birds of prey.

Cape serotine bat (*Eptesicus capensis*)

Yellow house bat (*Scotophilus dinganii*)

Distribution: This is one of the most common bats in the subregion. **Size:** Its forearm is 50-58mm whereas the Lesser house bat is slightly larger at 44-52mm. **Identification:** It is olive above and yellow on the belly. The yellow colour shows only when it is fully grown. Younger specimens may thus be confused with the lesser house bat. **Habitat:** It occurs in savanna woodland but is

Yellow house bat (*Scotophilus dinganii*)

often associated with houses where they may roost for the day. They prefer lower altitudes. **Habits:** They are gregarious, forming small groups of up to 12. **Food:** They are called aerial 'intermediate clutter feeders'. They feed on insects, medium-sized beetles and moths. **Reproduction:** They produce 1-3 young once per year.

Lesser yellow house bat (*Scotophilus viridus*)

Distribution: It is not as common as the Yellow house bat. **Description:** It is yellowish-brown above and the underparts are white or grey-white. Its forearm length is ±44-52mm, compared to 50-58mm in the House bat, *S.din-ganii*. **Habitat:** They occur in low-lying savanna woodland. **Habits:** They form small colonies. **Food:** They are intermediate fliers and intermediate clutter feeders, feeding on beetles, moths and other insects. **Reproduction:** They employ delayed implantation where the fertilised egg is implanted after hibernation with an effective gestation of 7,5 months. Implantation is delayed for half the winter period whereas in Schreiber's long-fingered bat (*Miniopterus schreibersii*), it is delayed for the whole winter.

Lesser yellow house bat (*Scotophilus viridus*)

Butterfly bat (*Chalinolobus variegatus*)

Description: Its colour is a light fawn to almost cream and the underside is even lighter. It can be distinguished by the dark reticulation on the wing. **Habitat:** It occurs in open savanna woodland. **Habits:** Butterfly bats form small colonies of ±10. **Food:** They are high to intermediate fliers and feed on insects, including moths. **Distribution:** They are quite rare.

Butterfly bat (*Chalinolobus variegatus*)

Schlieffen's bat (*Nycticeinops schlieffeni*)

Description: This bat is pale fawn above and paler below. Characteristic of this species is the darker brown wings. **Habitat:** It occurs in savanna woodland near pans or in riverine woodland. **Habits:** It is probably solitary but there is no definite data for southern Africa. **Feeding:** They are woodland edge feeders, feeding on insects such as beetles, moths, lacewings and *Hymenoptera*. **Reproduction:** Their gestation is 11 weeks and they breed only once per year. They have 1-3 young. Mating occurs in winter but

Schlieffens bat
(*Nycticeinops schlieffeni*)

they employ a different method than the delayed implantation of fertilised eggs (like that which occurs in the Lesser house bat and Schreiber's long-fingered bat). They store their sperm both in the male and the female reproductive tracts. Ovulation and fertilisation take place only in spring followed by the 11 week gestation.

HORSESHOE BATS
Order CHIROPTERA   Suborder MICROCHIROPTERA   Family RHINOLOPHIDAE

This group is so named because of the horseshoe shaped 'leaves' on their faces, which enhance their echolocation ability, enabling them to hunt in dense vegetation. The Darling's horseshoe bat employs a delayed reproductive method through sperm storage.

Hildebrandt's horseshoe bat
(*Rhinolophus hildebrandtii*)

Hildebrandt's horseshoe bat
(*Rhinolophus hildebrandtii*)

Description: This is the largest of the horseshoe bats. The 'horseshoe' is up to 9mm at its broadest part. The ears are sharply pointed and large. **Habitat:** It occurs in woodland savanna. **Food:** Manoevreable fliers that can forage in dense bush because of their enhanced echolocation ability (by means of the 'leaves' on the nose). They also do perch-hunting and gleaning. **Habits:** They form colonies of up to a few hundred. **Distribution:** They occur in the higher-rainfall north-eastern part of Southern Africa and are absent in the south-western arid regions.

Darling's horseshoe bat
(*Rhinolophus darlingi*)

Darling's horseshoe bat
(*Rhinolophus darlingi*)

Description: This bat has the characteristic horseshoe-shaped 'leaves' on the face. **Habitat:** It occurs in savanna woodland, preferring rocky terrain. **Habits:** They form colonies of ±20-40. **Breeding:** Delayed reproduction takes place in this species through sperm storage, the same as for Schlieffen's bat (*Nycticeinops schlieffeni*).

LEAF-NOSED BATS
Order CHIROPTERA   Suborder MICROCHIROPTERA   Family HIPPOSIDERIDAE

Like the horseshoe bats, these have a 'leafnose'. However, in this group it is simpler and especially so in the genus *Hipposideros*, where it has a simple elliptical shape.

Sundevall's leaf-nosed bat
(*Hipposideros caffer*)

Sundevall's leaf-nosed bat
(*Hipposideros caffer*)

Description: This is a very small bat with long, fluffy fur. The ears are broad and pointed and they have a pair of false nipples in the anal region of the female. **Habitat:** They occur in riverine woodland. **Habits:** They are gregarious, forming colonies of 100 or less. They roost hanging from their hind claws. **Food:** They are slow flyers and clutter feeders. They can also glean, feeding on moths, lacewings and other insects. **Reproduction:** Their gestation is 220 days (just over 7 months). They employ a form of delay, but in this case the delay is due to retarded embryonic growth, which occurs during hibernation. A single young is born in December. Normal fertilisation takes place in autumn.

SLIT-FACED BATS
Order CHIROPTERA   Suborder MICROCHIROPTERA   Family NYCTERIDAE

This family has a vertical split in the face where the 'noseleaves' occur. The latter play an important role in enhancing their echolocation ability. This makes them more manoeuvreable and enables them to forage in dense bush. Their ears are long (±3,5cm), making them easy to recognise. Another characteristic of this family is that the tails end in a t-shape where it meets the end of the tail membrane. It is supported by a spur.

Common slit-faced bat
(Nycteris thebaica)

Comon slit-faced bat
(*Nycteris thebaica*)

Description: This is one of the easiest bats to identify because of its long ears and the slit in the face. **Habitat:** They occur in open savanna woodland and are very widespread and common. They do not occur in the arid Kalahari regions of Botswana. Their day roosts are in caves, tree hollows, roofs and even aardvark holes. Their night roosts are often in roof overhangs. **Habits:** They occur in small colonies of ±5. In Drotsky's caves in Botswana, there are colonies of up to 600. **Food:** They are capable of slow flight and are predominantly gleaners, gleaning their food both from vegetation and from the ground. Their long ears ensure accurate hearing and they often react to insect sounds and movement on the ground. The split in the face enhances their echolocation ability, making it possible for them to forage in dense bush. **Reproduction:** They have a gestation of five months and a single young is born. There is no known reproductive delay mechanism in this species.

BIBLIOGRAPHY

Apps, P. (1992) *Wild Ways - Field Guide to the Behaviour of Southern African Mammals*, Southern Book Publishers, Halfway House, Johannesburg, South Africa, 1992.

Bothma, J. du P. (1996) *Game Ranch Management*, J.L. van Schaik Publishers, Pretoria, South Africa.

Carnaby, Trevor (2006) *Beat About the Bush - Mammals*, Jacana media, Johannesburg, South Africa.

Cillie, Burger (2004) *The Mammal Guide of Southern Africa*, Briza Publications, Pretoria, South Africa, 2004.

Cole, Desmond T. (1995) *Setswana - Animals and Plants*, Botswana Society, Gaborone, Botswana.

Comley, P. and Meyer, S. (1994) *A Field Guide to the mammals of Botswana*, Hirt & Carter, (Pty) Ltd, Durban, SA.

De Blase, F & Martin, R.E. (1982) *A Mannual of Mammalogy*, Wm. C. Brown Company Publisher, Iowa, USA.

De Graaff, G (1981) *The Rodents of Southern Africa*, Butterworth & CO (SA) (Pty) Ltd, Durban, South Africa.

Eltringham, S.K. (1990) *The Illustrated Encyclopedia of Elephants*, Salamander Books Ltd., London, England.

Estes, Richard D. (1992) *The Behaviour Guide to African Mammals*, University of California Press, USA.

Goraon, S. et.al. (1982) *Animal Physiology - Principles and Adaptations*, Macmillan Publishing Co., New York. USA.

Hildebrand, Milton (1988) *Analysis of Vertebrate Structure, Third Edition*, John Wiley and Sons, USA / Canada.

Kingdon, Jonathan (1989) *East African mammals Volume IIIA, Carnivores*, University of Chicago Press.

Kingdon, Jonathan (1989) *East African mammals Volume IIIB, Large Mammals*, University of Chicago Press.

Kingdon, Jonathan (1989) *East African mammals Volume IIIB, Bovids*, University of Chicago Press.

Kingdon, Jonathan (1989) *East African mammals Volume IIIC, Bovids*, University of Chicago Press.

Kingdon, Jonathan (1997) *The Kingdon Field Guide to African Mmmals*, Academic Press, San Diego, USA, 1997.

Liebenberg, Louis (1990) *A Field Guide to the Animal Tracks of Southern Africa*, David Philip Publishers (Pty) Ltd, Clairmont, SA.

Louw, Gideon (1993) *Physiological Animal Ecology*, Longman Scientific and Techncal, Harlow, Essex, England.

Lovegrove, Barry (1993) *The Living Deserts of Southern Africa*, Fernwood Press, Vlaeberg, South Africa.

Reader's Digest, Mc Bride G. & Berrill, N.J. (1974) *Animal Families*, Reader's Digest Far East Limited, Hong Kong.

Saunders, J.T. and Manton, S.M. (1969) *A Manual of Practical Vertebrate Morphology*, Oxford University Press, England.

Schmidt-Nielsen, K. (1998) *Animal Physiology*, Cambridge University Press, New York, USA.

Skinner, J.D. & Smithers, R.H.N (1990) *The Mammals of the Sothern African Subregon*, University of Pretoria, Pretoria, South Africa.

Smithers, Reay.H.N. (1992) *Land mammals of Southern Africa - A Field Guide*, Southern Book Publishers, Halfway House, Johannesburg, South Africa.

Spinage, C.A (1986) *The Natural History of Antelopes*, Croom Helm Publishers, Beckenham, Kent, UK.

Taylor, P.J. (2000) *Bats of Southern Africa*, University of Natal Press, Scotsville, South Africa.

INDEX